GE
LOCOMOTIVES
110 YEARS OF GENERAL ELECTRIC MOTIVE POWER

Brian Solomon

MBI

Dedication
To my friends Tim Doherty and Patrick Yough

This edition first published in 2003 by MBI Publishing Company, Galtier Plaza, Suite 200, 380 Jackson Street, St. Paul, MN 55101-3885 USA

MBI Publishing Company titles are also available at discounts in bulk quantity for industrial or sales-promotional use. For details write to Special Sales Manager at Motorbooks International Wholesalers & Distributors, Galtier Plaza, Suite 200, 380 Jackson Street, St. Paul, MN 55101-3885 USA.

Library of Congress Cataloging-in-Publication Data

Solomon, Brian
    GE locomotives / by Brian Solomon
        p. cm.
    ISBN 0-7603-1361-X (hc. : alk. paper)
    1. Diesel locomotives--United States. 2. General Electric
        Company. I. Title.
    TJ619.2.S652 2003
    625.26'62'0973--dc21

On the front cover: In the summer evening glow, Burlington Northern westbound freights wait on the Montana Rail Link at Helena, Montana. To the west lies the crossing of the Continental Divide at Mullen Pass. Locomotive 8592 is a B39-8 leased to Burlington Northern from GE's lease-fleet subsidiary, LMX, on a "power by the hour" basis. The LMX locomotives were often assigned to intermodal services and are frequently operated with BN's 12-cylinder B30-7AB cabless units. *Brian Solomon*

On the frontispiece: CSX C30-7 No. 7001 displays the classic cab used by GE on most domestic Universal Line and Series 7 production locomotives. In 2002 this locomotive was serving in work train service in West Virginia. *Brian Solomon*

On the title page: On February 19, 1995, in a scene symbolic of the competitive American locomotive market, GECX lease-fleet B39-8 No. 8000, dressed in GE company colors, leads a Burlington Northern intermodal train eastbound through Rochelle, Illinois, past EMD's BL20 demonstrator, which sits on a siding. *Brian Solomon*

On the Contents page: Three Erie-Lackawanna U33Cs lead a westbound Delaware & Hudson freight at East Worcester, New York, on March 31, 1969. *Jim Shaughnessy*

On the Acknowledgments page: The DASH 9 line was introduced shortly before General Electric's AC-traction locomotives and represented the most advanced GE DC-traction design. DASH 9 and AC4400CW production was concurrent, with both locomotives being built side by side at Erie. On November 6, 1994, Southern Pacific DASH 9-44CW No. 8110 is seen against the silhouette of the setting sun. *Brian Solomon*

On the Introduction page: A Burlington Northern Santa Fe DASH 9-44CW and two Santa Fe–painted DASH 8s lead an eastbound double-stack container train over the Belen Cutoff near Abo Canyon, New Mexico, in September 1998. *Brian Solomon*

On the back cover: In 1995, General Electric began delivering "convertible" AC6000CWs to Union Pacific. These locomotives featured the larger platform designed for the new 6,000-horsepower 7HDL-16 engine, but were powered by GE's traditional 7FDL-16 and rated at just 4,400 horsepower. Union Pacific 7026 looms out of the setting sun at Colo, Iowa, on the former Chicago & North Western mainline. *Brian Solomon*

Edited by Dennis Pernu
Designed by LeAnn Kuhlmann

Printed in China

CONTENTS

ACKNOWLEDGMENTS

My experience with General Electric locomotives dates from a very early age. I was barely two years old when I watched New York Central U25Bs working the West Side Line pass beneath the grates in Manhattan's Riverside Park. I recall a New Haven/Penn Central EP-5 electric roaring into a station in Connecticut, and I have many fond recollections of former Pennsylvania Railroad GG1 electrics—some of which were built in part by General Electric. In 1980, my father and I enjoyed a pleasant cab ride on a GE 70-tonner, courtesy of the Belfast & Moosehead Lake. In later years, I spent many days photographing trains along the old Boston & Albany line, a route that was populated with a variety of General Electric diesels.

Since then, I have traveled widely and photographed General Electric products in a great many settings. I could not have had these experiences without the help and guidance of many different people. My father, Richard Jay Solomon, focused my early interests in railways. In more recent times his extensive library of railroad publications has proved invaluable in my research. Many of his photographs of GE electrics appear in this book. My grandparents, Alfred and Bessie Solomon, had a wonderful veranda in The Bronx, from which my brother Seán and I watched many trains led by GE electrics and diesels. My mother, Maureen, also contributed in many ways.

Robert A. Buck of Tucker's Hobbies in Warren, Massachusetts, has been a great supporter of my railroad interest and a source of stories and information over the years. Many locomotive engineers have lent their expertise and opinions on locomotive operation and performance; among them are Robert Foreman, Craig Willett, and Steve Carlson. Special thanks to the kind Conrail engineer who, in the summer of 1984, gave a friend and me an unforgettable cab ride on C30-7A 6597. Thomas M. Hoover helped me better understand the intricacies of the 7FDL engine and the particulars of the Dash-7 line. William S. Young enlightened me on details of GE's 70-ton diesels, and Bill Kratville was especially helpful with research on General Electric turbine locomotives. Thanks to Tom Tancula and the staff at Eesti Raudtee for their hospitality and cooperation in Estonia. It was a privilege and a thrill to experience big GEs in action on 5-foot-gauge tracks. The Irish Railway Record Society was very generous with its extensive library of railway literature.

I often travel with other photographers, and they have contributed in many ways in the making of the images that appear in this book. Thanks to Brian Jennison, J.D. Schmid, T.S. Hoover, Mel Patrick, Mike Gardner, Don Marson, George S. Pitarys, Blair Koostra, Brandon Delany, Joe Snopek, Mike Abalos, Jon Roma, Brian Plant, Pete Ruesch, Brad Hellman, Scott Bontz, Dave Burton, Dave Stanley, Mike Valentine, Mark Hemphill, Mike Danneman, Tom Danneman, Hal Miller, Howard Ande, Joe McMillan, Don Gulbrandsen, Carl Swanson, F.L. Becht, Gerald Hook, Danny Johnson, Brian Rutherford, Vic Neves, David Monte Verde, Dean Sauvola, Mark Leppert, John Peters, Norman Yellin, Tim Hensch, Marshall Beecher, Mike Schafer, Doug Moore, and Doug Eisele. Some of their photos are reproduced here, and each is credited appropriately.

Thanks also to Tom Kline, Doug Koontz, Jeremy Plant, John Leopard, Eric T. Hendrickson, the Denver Public Library, and the Smithsonian Institution for supplying photos for this project, and to Mike Gardner for the extensive use of his black-and-white darkroom facilities. Special thanks to Jim Shaughnessy and William D. Middleton for their generosity in supplying historical and contemporary images. In addition, William D. Middleton offered his expertise on electric locomotives. Thanks to Tim Doherty for photographic support and help with research and questions, and to Patrick Yough for research, help with captions, photographs, and insights on GE operation on Metro-North. John Gruber helped with research, supplied historical photos, and wrote two sidebars that add breadth to the text.

My interest in locomotives was inspired by fellow authors and locomotive enthusiasts. My dad's original copy of Louis A. Marre and Jerry A. Pinkepank's first *Diesel Spotter's Guide* is in tatters from excessive perusal, and over the years I've learned much from both writers. As the editor of *Pacific RailNews*, I met Sean Graham-White and have worked with him on several occasions. He is one of the most knowledgeable authors on modern diesel locomotives. Numerous informative articles on modern locomotives have also appeared in the pages of *TRAINS Magazine*. Jay Potter is an author whom I admire for his detailed writing of modern diesel operations. Articles and books by Greg McDonnell, Bill Kratville, and John F. Kirkland have also been enjoyable and educational.

Special thanks to my editor at MBI, Dennis Pernu, and to everyone else at MBI who assisted in layout, design, and production. Last, thanks to all the employees of General Electric who have designed and built the many fine locomotives portrayed.

INTRODUCTION

General Electric's locomotive development is an important aspect in modern American railway history and railway locomotion has been a part of the company's business since its inception in the 1890s. GE has pioneered much of the technology employed in modern locomotive design, and today is one of the best-known and largest producers of locomotives worldwide. In assembling this book, I have read through hundreds of documents, articles, and books on many aspects of locomotive technology, application, and business. I've distilled this vast array of information and attempted to portray General Electric's locomotives in a logical, comprehendible manner. Listing technical specifications should allow practical comparison of different models and will hopefully enable a better understanding of each type. In addition to discussing the development of locomotive technology, competition within the business, and relevant statistics of various types of locomotives, I've described the jobs locomotives do, their appearances, and significant or distinguishing characteristics of different models. I've made every effort to publish accurate information, and often worked from official sources. In some cases I have found incongruent information; in these situations I list more than one set of figures and attribute the source of each respectively.

This book is intended as a gallery of GE locomotives and not as an encyclopedia. I have divided it into nine chapters, each of which focuses on different loco-motive lines. I have no doubt that each chapter could easily be expanded into a book on its own. General Electric has produced many thousands of locomotives over the course of 110 years, and it is often necessary to generalize discussion of different types. While touching on a great many different machines, I have highlighted specific models that I feel are historically significant and may thus be of greater interest to the reader. Some models, which could have been discussed in greater detail, may only get a passing mention. This text is not intended as critical discussion of specific locomotive reliability and performance. Instead, I've illustrated how General Electric has consistently attempted to en-gineer better technology in order to secure a larger market share and provide better machines for its cus-tomers. However, I discuss some machines' perceived inadequacies to help the reader understand why certain types enjoyed only limited application or unusually short service lives. I am not qualified to provide a de-tailed, unbiased analysis of locomotive performance and reliability, nor do I feel that such an analysis would be appropriate for this text.

One of my specialties is photography, and I have gone to great lengths to produce and procure the best possible images. I have spent more than 20 years pho-tographing railways and have often focused my lenses on General Electric products. I consider myself fortu-nate to have witnessed hundreds of General Electric locomotives in action in numerous interesting settings. Combining my interests has enabled me to produce unique and distinctive images. In selecting photo-graphs, I've poured over tens of thousands of images. In addition to my own extensive files and those of my father, I reviewed photographs from dozens of other sources. I've tried to pick photographs that best illus-trate the variety of machines described in the text, while showing locomotives in a positive light. In addi-tion, I've illustrated GE locomotives in their working environments, and have not focused strictly on the hardware.

Appreciation of photography is entirely subjective, but I hope that the images portrayed here convey my fascination and admiration for the majesty of these great machines.

—*Brian Solomon, Dublin 2002*

ELECTRIC LOCOMOTIVES

The emergence of commercial electric enterprise in the 1870s and 1880s made possible a whole new form of railway motive power. The prospects of developing and selling electric railway propulsion intrigued electrical pioneers. Railways were among the biggest businesses at the time, and railway applications were one of the first large markets for electrical technology.

In the decades before the development of commercial electrical power grids, electric railways provided a base for experimentation and demonstration. Experiments in electric railway propulsion had been undertaken as early as the 1830s, using battery-powered miniature locomotives. In 1879, Werner Von Siemens exhibited a small electric railway in Berlin, marking the first practical public demonstration of an electric locomotive powered by a generator, or—as they called it then—a dynamo. Inspired by this, General Electric's founder, Thomas A. Edison, began experimenting with electric railway propulsion in 1880. Following initial testing on a very short segment, Edison conducted more extensive experiments at the behest of Northern Pacific's Henry Villiard, using a test track 2-1/4 miles long. This track, like the first, was located in Menlo Park, New Jersey. According to *Railway Wonders of the World*, published around 1914, Edison built a small standard gauge electric locomotive sufficiently powerful to haul three cars.

CHAPTER 1

Opposite: The New Haven Railroad pioneered mainline electrification. Its first electrified route from New York to Cos Cob, Connecticut, began regular service in June 1907. On June 28, 1958, an unusually painted New Haven EP-3 electric leads train No. 145 westbound at Stamford, Connecticut. General Electric built the New Haven's 10 EP-3s in 1931. They used a 2-C+C-2 wheel arrangement and inspired the Pennsylvania Railroad's GG1 electric design of 1934. *Richard Jay Solomon*

General Electric's first double-truck electric locomotive (and its second locomotive) was built in 1894 for the Cayadutta Railway and spent most of its working life at a cotton mill in Taftville, Connecticut. GE classified the locomotive as Type 404-E70-4 LWP 20-500 volts. Significantly, it used nose-suspended traction motors, the arrangement that became standard on nearly all diesel-electric locomotives. *Duke-Middleton collection, photographer unknown*

By the early 1890s, American engineers, including Leo Daft, Stephen Field, and Frank J. Sprague, were among the world leaders in the development of electric railway technology. Sprague, a onetime employee of Edison, was an inventor responsible for many important innovations in electric railway technology, including the first large-scale applications of electric propulsion, on the Richmond Union Passenger Railway in Virginia in 1888. Sprague's company became part of Edison-GE in 1890. Following this success,

numerous horse-drawn street railway lines in the United States and other parts of the world were electrified. The electrically powered trolley car became a symbol of progress. More than 850 electric street railway systems were operational by 1898, and just about every self-respecting city or town had invested in electric trolleys.

A spinoff of the electric street railway was the electric interurban line, which connected cities and towns and by the first decade of the twentieth century in almost every region in the United States. In general, these electric lines, including their track and roadbeds, were built to much lower standards than conventional steam-powered railways. Their cars were also smaller and lighter than were those on steam trains. Interurbans competed directly with the steam railways for passenger traffic and, in some cases, freight. General Electric was a primary supplier of electrical gear used on street and interurban railways, and supported electrical infrastructure, such as the power stations and substations needed to generate and transmit electricity.

General Electric was also a pioneer in the construction of electric locomotives. In 1893 at its Lynn, Massachusetts, facility, GE built its first commercial electric locomotive for steam railway service. In his book, *When the Steam Railroads Electrified*, William D. Middleton describes it as a 30-ton, four-wheel machine, capable of 30 miles per hour. GE built a second, larger locomotive in 1894. Middleton indicates that this steeple cab was 24 feet long, weighed 35 tons, and rode on a pair of twin-axle trucks powered by nose-suspended traction motors of a type developed by Sprague. This locomotive is of interest today because its double-truck design set an important precedent, and its nose-suspended traction motors were the prototypes for those used by GE's later electrics and nearly all modern diesel-electric locomotives. (A nose-suspended motor is supported on one end by the axle and on other end by the truck frame. It typically uses single-reduction gearing to power the axle.) This original steeple cab had an extraordinarily long career working a cotton mill in Taftville, Connecticut. It was retired in 1964 and today is displayed at the Connecticut Trolley Museum at Warehouse Point, Connecticut. Steeple-cab electrics of a similar design became a standard type built by General Electric and were used by electric railways for many years.

The Pros and Cons of Electrification

Heavy railway electrification was a logical outgrowth of street railway and interurban electrification, although railroads were slow to explore its potential. The earliest electric

This photograph, made July 22, 1894, shows one of the Cayadutta Railway locomotive trucks that featured nose-suspended traction motors, a standard arrangement on electric trolley cars of the period. General Electric's early nose-suspended motors were the technological predecessors to the successful DC motors used by most diesel-electric manufacturers. *Duke-Middleton collection, photographer unknown*

General Electric pioneered heavy railroad electrification when it contracted to electrify Baltimore & Ohio's new Howard Street Tunnel in 1892. Electric service began in 1895. In this period photo, B&O electric No. 1 poses beyond the south portal of the tunnel, near the railroad's Camden Station in Baltimore. In the first few years, B&O electric locomotives took power from a rigid overhead system, seen here above the locomotive. After 1900, a more conventional outside third-rail replaced the overhead system. *Industrial Photo Service, William D. Middleton collection*

propulsion systems were not powerful enough to power mainline trains, although in the mid-1890s the New Haven and Pennsylvania railroads experimented with short electrified sections akin to trolley lines.

The prospects of major steam railway electrification generated considerable controversy during the last decade of the nineteenth century and the first decades of the twentieth. Proponents of electrification claimed numerous potential advantages. Electrification was a more efficient use of energy and could lower fuel and maintenance costs. Electric motors also provided greater starting power than steam power. Electrified operations could lower labor costs and simplify operations by using double-ended equipment and eliminating fuel and water stops required by steam

engines. However, the most conspicuous advantages of electrification from the public viewpoint were significantly cleaner and quieter trains. Coal-burning steam locomotives are dirty machines that belch smoke, leaving a layer of soot on everything they pass. These latter considerations, as much as operational efficiency, encouraged the installation of America's first heavy-duty electrification.

Despite the many prospective advantages of electrification, railroads observed the developing technology cautiously. In the 1890s, a lack of suitable technology for heavy railroad operations precluded serious investment. The high initial costs of electrification were difficult for railroads to justify, despite the allure of lower operating costs. In addition to the great expense of electrical supply equipment and

Between 1903 and 1906, General Electric built five boxcab electrics for Baltimore & Ohio's Howard Street Tunnel electrification. These B&O boxcabs, Nos. 7, 6, and 9, lead a freight in about 1915. Electrics would haul trains, complete with steam locomotive, through the tunnel to avoid smoke problems. Notice the brakemen riding on the freight cars. *Smithsonian Institution Neg. No. 49870, courtesy of William D. Middleton*

specialized locomotives, electrification required separate shops and specially trained mechanics to maintain the equipment. Other costs included expensive signaling equipment that was shielded from interference with its electrical transmissions. Safety concerns due to hazards posed by high-voltage lines also fueled electrification opponents. The specialized and somewhat inflexible equipment imposed operational constraints.

First Mainline Electrification

By the 1880s, America's first public railway, the Baltimore & Ohio, was moving a vast quantity of freight and passengers through its namesake port. It was also looking to improve its route through Baltimore to better compete with the Pennsylvania Railroad, which had just completed its through line across that city. Saddled with complex terminal arrangements that made the operation of through trains slow and difficult, B&O planned a new "Belt Line" through Baltimore that included a long tunnel beneath a residential area of downtown. The railroad faced serious public opposition to its plan, as residents were appalled at the thought of

steam trains spreading foul smoke and soot as they passed under vents near their homes. To overcome an impasse over the proposed tunnel, B&O made the unprecedented decision to electrify.

The railroad turned to General Electric for equipment and locomotives to electrify the Belt Line, which included the new 1-1/4-mile Howard Street Tunnel and a new passenger station and shed at Mt. Royal. Today, this may seem like a logical solution to a difficult problem, but at the time it was a bold step. Despite the growing number of lightweight electric street railways and a few branchline experiments, up until then no railway in the world had attempted to electrify a full-scale mainline operation.

The first electric operations began at the end of June 1895, and regular operations began in July. The electrified section was very short, a little more than 3 miles of mainline. The system of electrification was derived from the 600-volt direct current systems employed by most contemporary street railways, but required a substantially heavier delivery mechanism than provided by lightweight overhead trolley wire. The voltage was 675 volts (some sources indicate 650 volts); instead of wire, General Electric devised a peculiar rigid overhead electrical supply system. Locomotives drew power from the overhead rail using an angled, flexible pantograph fixed to the locomotive on its bottom and gripping the rail with a brass fitting. Initially, the B&O used three steeple-cab locomotives built by GE at Schenectady, New York. Each locomotive weighed about 192,000 pounds, making them much heavier than typical steam locomotives of the period. Brian Hollingsworth points out in *The Illustrated Encyclopedia of North American Locomotives* that the first B&O electrics were nine times heavier than any other electrics operating at that time. Each was designed to haul a train weighing up to 1,870 tons up the 0.8 percent grade in the Howard Street Tunnel. Propulsion was provided by four gearless, 360-horsepower direct current electric motors. Motor armatures engaged hollow quills that surrounded the driving axles, and the quills connected to 62-inch spoked driving wheels using rubber blocks. The blocks provided a flexible connection that cushioned shocks to the motors.

Electric locomotives hauled trains, steam locomotives and all, through the tunnel. (Leaving the regular road locomotive on its train reduced transit delays.) Since the steam locomotive did not have to work in the tunnel, smoke emissions were minimal. When the train reached the end of the electrified section, the electric locomotive would be cut off and switched out of the way, and the steam locomotive would take over again.

The electrics proved a practical motive power solution, though the electrical distribution was awkward. After 1900, B&O replaced the fixed overhead system with a more suitable ground-level, overrunning third-rail, similar to that used on the newly electrified New York City elevated rapid transit lines. Baltimore & Ohio's pioneering electrification, America's only significant mainline electric operation for the better part of a decade, set important precedents for later electric operations.

Baltimore & Ohio bought additional electric locomotives from General Electric between 1909 and 1912. These more modern machines, Classes OE-1 and OE-2, were of a boxcab design and allowed B&O to retire its pioneer steeple cabs. Between 1923 and 1927, B&O added more GE locomotives, Classes OE-3 and OE-4. These brought back the center-cab design, with a B-B wheel arrangement.

The OE-4 employed four GE 209C traction motors that developed 1,100 horsepower. The locomotive was 41 feet, 4 inches long and 14 feet, 3-1/2 inches tall (including headlamps). It weighed 242,000 pounds and could deliver 60,500 pounds starting tractive effort. The advent of modern diesel-electrics negated the need for the Baltimore Belt Line electrification, and Baltimore & Ohio discontinued electric operations in the early 1950s.

New York's Grand Central Quandary

At the end of the nineteenth century, New York City was the largest city in the United States and its population was growing rapidly. Suburban railways that fed Manhattan allowed

GE built New York Central's Class R-2 electrics for the railroad's West Side electrification in Manhattan. General Electric designated these locomotives C+C-270/270-6GE286. Although the C-C wheel arrangement was unusual in 1930 and 1931 when they were built, it has since become the standard wheel arrangement used by American diesel-electrics in freight service. *General Electric photo, William D. Middleton collection*

General Electric sold electrification systems, including power-generating systems, substations, and locomotives. This GE rotary converter located in a substation at East Troy, Wisconsin, was used to convert high-voltage AC power into low-voltage DC for The Milwaukee Electric Railway & Light Company. *Brian Solomon*

workers to live much farther from the city than was possible in earlier times. While numerous railway lines served the New York area, most reached Manhattan by way of ferry connections. The only direct passenger route was New York Central's Park Avenue Tunnel to Grand Central Depot, a station that it shared with the New York, New Haven & Hartford Railroad. The latter utilized trackage rights over New York Central between Woodlawn Junction in The Bronx and Grand Central. Between the two railroads, some 500 daily trains served Grand Central, making it among the busiest stations in the world.

New York Central enlarged Grand Central in 1898 to accommodate the growing tide of passenger traffic, but even as the enlargement was being completed, it recognized the inadequacies of the new station and started investigating the construction of an entirely new terminal on the site. Capacity was a primary concern. Even in the 1890s, Manhattan real estate was expensive, putting serious space constraints on the terminal and making expansion difficult. As a result, the railroad needed to make the maximum use of the space. According to William D. Middleton in his

book, *Grand Central: The World's Greatest Railway Terminal*, in 1899, William J. Wilgus, New York Central vice president and chief engineer, envisioned a two-level underground terminal station. However, this novel solution was not possible with conventional steam power because of smoke. As it was, the existing station suffered badly from smoke, and locomotives were kept outside the station shed until they were needed to move trains. Wilgus' concept would be practical only if the new station was electrified. And so, envisioning an electrified suburban railway system for New York, Wilgus met with electric traction pioneer Frank J. Sprague to discuss the possibilities of electrifying Grand Central. Nothing like this had ever been accomplished on such a grand scale. While Wilgus was pondering the potentials of electrification, a horrible disaster propelled the railroad to the forefront of electric railway technology.

Trains to Grand Central traversed deep cuts and a long tunnel below Park Avenue. At times of peak traffic, smoke made it difficult for locomotive engineers to see line-side signals that governed train movements. On the morning of January 8, 1902, an inbound New York Central

passenger train approaching Grand Central overran a stop signal obscured by smoke and collided at speed with a standing New Haven suburban train waiting for permission to enter the station. The collision splintered fragile wooden passenger cars and when the smoke cleared, 15 people were dead and many others seriously injured. While rear-end collisions were a common accident in those days, because this disaster occurred in Manhattan, it was sensationalized by the media, resulting in a tide of public outrage. The fury fueled legislation that effectively banned steam locomotive operation in Manhattan. In effect, these laws precipitated some of the most significant motive power developments in American railroad history, as New York City's railroads were forced to develop a whole new magnitude of electric railway technology.

To meet the challenge set by state lawmakers, the Central established the Electric Traction Commission (ETC)—a think tank of the nation's foremost experts on electrical engineering, including Wilgus, Sprague, and George Gibbs. By studying previous applications of electric railway traction on street railways—namely the Baltimore & Ohio's 1895 electrification and recent third-rail electrifications on elevated rapid transit lines in Manhattan, Brooklyn, and Chicago—the ETC concluded that a 660-volt, direct current system delivered by outside third-rail was the most appropriate for the railroad's needs.

In the 1890s, there had been great discussion about the virtues and disadvantages of direct current (DC) and alternating current (AC) electrification schemes, not just for railway traction, but for general power distribution. The advantages of DC were its overall simplicity and ease of motor control. Disadvantages were inefficiency of long-distance transmission, requiring frequent and expensive electrical substations to provided adequate power. Direct current

worked well on electric street railways, where short distances and light vehicle weights were predominant. General Electric had promoted DC electrification, while Westinghouse favored AC schemes, but in 1896 the two companies agreed on a patent exchange that facilitated the manufacture of either technology by either company. Despite this exchange, GE continued to promote DC, while Westinghouse went on to pioneer early high-voltage AC transmission. New York Central selected a DC system, which was the best developed for railway applications at the time. Logically, the Schenectady, New York–based General Electric was chosen as its main supplier.

In 1895, GE's competitor, Westinghouse, had teamed up with Baldwin to build electric locomotives. (Both Westinghouse and Baldwin were Pennsylvania-based companies.) Baldwin manufactured mechanical components and Westinghouse supplied electrical gear. In response, GE teamed up with Alco in the construction of electric locomotives. Conveniently, GE and Alco both had primary manufacturing facilities at Schenectady. Later, GE and

Alco became closely involved in the manufacture of diesels. Baldwin and Westinghouse were similarly linked, and in 1948 Westinghouse took control of its longtime locomotive-building partner.

New York Central's First Electric

A formal arrangement between GE and Alco was still a couple of years away when New York Central contracted with GE for a prototype locomotive in anticipation of its Grand Central electrification. Working with New York Central's Electric Traction Commission in 1904, GE designed and built No. 6000, a double-ended machine with a 1-D-1 wheel arrangement. (Powered axles are counted in groups represented by a letter: A for one axle, B for two, C for three, etc. Numbers indicate unpowered axles. Hence, No. 6000 had four powered axles between two unpowered axles.) It employed a center-cab configuration, a common arrangement on many early electrics. As the 6000 was intended to haul New York Central's fast express trains, it needed the same capabilities as Central's state-of-the-art passenger

steam locomotives. Four 550-horsepower bi-polar (two pole) traction motors produced a total continuous output of 2,200 horsepower and were capable of a short-term output of up to 3,000 horsepower. It used a gearless traction motor design, in which motor poles were mounted on the locomotive frame and armatures directly on the axles. Both poles and armatures were spring-loaded to maintain flexibility. According to Brian Hollingsworth in *The Illustrated Encyclopedia of North American Locomotives*, the total locomotive weight was 200,500 pounds, with approximately 142,000 pounds on driving wheels, giving the machine a maximum axle load of about 35,500 pounds. The locomotive was designed to haul a standard 450-ton passenger train and was capable of hauling trains weighing almost twice that amount.

The 6000 set many precedents that were copied and improved upon in later locomotives. Its design was largely the work of GE's Asa Batchelder, but it also incorporated important innovations designed by Sprague. Perhaps most significant was the first use of Sprague's electro-pneumatic multiple-unit (MU) control system on a locomotive. Sprague's MU control was developed in 1897 to allow two or more electric units (railcars or, in this case, locomotives) to be operated synchronously under the control of a single engineer (operator). This pioneering use of MU control has significant historical precedent. Nearly all diesel-electric locomotives today are built with MU controls and it is standard practice to operate locomotives in multiple. The ability to operate multiple electric, and subsequently diesel-electric,

Continued on page 24

One of the most ambitious American mainline electrification schemes was the wiring of Milwaukee Road's Pacific Extension. One of Milwaukee's massive EP-2 "Bi-Polar" electrics is seen with train No. 17, the westbound *Columbian*. This July 11, 1925, photo features the railroad's Washington State electrification west of Rockdale Yard on Snoqualmie Pass. *Asamel Curtis, Washington State Historical Society, courtesy of William D. Middleton*

Above: Three-phase AC-traction diesel-electrics are commonplace today, but GE was building them long before modern diesels. In 1911, GE electrified Great Northern's Cascade crossing at Stevens Pass using a 6,600-volt, three-phase overhead system that required two sets of delivery wires. The electric locomotives, such as these seen at Tye, Washington, in May 1915, used four GE-1506 induction traction motors to produce a total of 1,500 horsepower. In the 1920s, Great Northern relocated its Cascade crossing and re-electrified it, using a more conventional 11,000-volt, single-phase AC system. *Asamel Curtis, Washington State Historical Society, courtesy of William D. Middleton*

Opposite: In 1947, General Electric built two massive streamlined motor-generator electrics for Great Northern. Rated at 5,000 horsepower, they were the largest electrics in the world at that time. Here, GN No. 4933 leads a freight train through the Cascades near Leavenworth, Washington. *Great Northern Railway photo, William D. Middleton collection*

Opposite, inset: The running gear for one of Great Northern's 360-ton electrics is seen on the shop floor at Erie, Pennsylvania, on January 28, 1947. GE classified these monster electrics as B-D+D-B-720/720-12GE745. All axles on this machine were powered by GE-745 traction motors. *Great Northern Railway photo, William D. Middleton collection*

Continued from page 21

locomotives was one of the great advantages of electric motive power over steam, dramatically increasing the amount of work one person could do.

Initially, NYC No. 6000 was listed as Class L, but was soon changed to Class T. Following later modifications, it was again changed to Class S. Locomotive 6000, later renumbered 100, was the railroad's sole S-1 electric. In 1905, it was used in extensive experiments on a 6-mile electrified test track parallel to New York Central's Water Level Route mainline in the shadow of GE's plant at Schenectady. To determine its full capabilities and to demonstrate the potential of electric traction, No. 6000 hauled trains of various weights back and forth on the test track. Although fairly level, portions of the line climbed a nominal grade of 0.36 percent. With a heavily loaded train, the locomotive accelerated to a speed of 65 miles per hour; in one test, 6000 is reported to have hauled a single coach at a speed of 79 miles per hour. Running light, it was capable of speeds of over 80 miles per hour, and is reported to have briefly attained 85 miles per hour.

No. 6000 was built during a period when publicity stunts were popular in America, and New York Central's George Daniels, the railroad's "general passenger agent," made the railroad's trains famous by staging widely publicized high-speed runs. The best remembered of these took place on May 10, 1893, when Daniels caught the world's eye with the record run of the *Empire State Express* behind 4-4-0 No. 999, a locomotive specially equipped with 7-foot-tall driving wheels for fast running. On that day, 999 is reported to have attained the improbable high speed of 112-1/2 miles per hour west of Batavia, New York.

As part of the 1905 experiments, New York Central staged races between its best steam power and its experimental electric, the results of which were published in *Railway Wonders of the World* (1914). At the time of the tests, one of New York Central's fastest and most modern passenger locomotives was the Pacific-type 4-6-2 No. 2799, built by Alco-Schenectady in 1903. According to Al Staufer in *New York Central's Later Power*, this locomotive featured 22x26-inch cylinders and 75-inch driving wheels, placed 140,000 pounds on drivers, and could deliver

28,500 pounds tractive effort. No. 2799 and No. 6000 were assigned to comparable passenger trains, taking into account the minor differences in locomotive weight, and raced against one another along the test track section of Central's mainline.

In the early tests it was found that the steam locomotive accelerated faster because initial voltage drops affected the electric's ability to gain speed. Once the electric got moving, however, it quickly overtook the Pacific, thus proving to ob- servers the viability and superiority of electric motive power. In one test, it took No. 6000 just 127 seconds to accelerate its train to 50 miles per hour, which was 76 seconds faster than the Pacific. New York Central also ran the electric in deep snow to demonstrate that it was an all-weather machine. Satisfied with the capabilities of the electric, New York Central ordered a fleet of 34 similar electrics from GE for its express and long-distance passenger service to Grand Central. These were originally classed as T-2, but were soon

On February 3, 1959, New Haven EP-4 No. 360 leads a train toward Penn Station through Sunnyside Yard in Queens, New York. In 1938, General Electric built 10 EP-4 electrics for New Haven Railroad based on the earlier EP-3 boxcab. *Richard Jay Solomon*

reclassified as S-2. The majority of Central's suburban services were handled by electric multiple units (self-propelled passenger cars) instead of locomotive-hauled trains.

Although New York Central was undertaking ambitious plans for an all-new Grand Central Terminal, it had to comply with a ban on steam power that went into effect July 1, 1908. As a result, the old Grand Central was electrified as an interim operation while the new terminal was built around it. The first electric services began on September 20, 1906, and by 1907 the station was mostly electrified. Initially, electric services only extended a few miles beyond Manhattan, but Central gradually extended the electrification to take better advantage of electric power and minimize the need for engine changes. By the mid-1920s, the third-rail extended 33 miles north of Grand Central to Croton-on-Hudson (now known as Croton-Harmon) on its famous Hudson Division, to North White Plains on its Harlem Division, and on the Getty Square Branch of its Putnam Division. In the 1930s, Central electrified its West Side freight line in Manhattan.

Shortly after the initiation of electric service, a second disastrous accident occurred when a train derailed at speed, killing 23 people. The tragic irony of the accident was that it demonstrated the fallibility of the new electric service that

had been introduced in specific response to the 1902 crash. The second disaster, like the first, had serious repercussions. Wilgus resigned, and New York Central was forced to re-evaluate the design of its electric locomotives. Sensational press reports propelled technical details of railway operation into public consciousness and resulted in a greater demand for safety. New York Central took action by rebuilding all of its electrics with leading bogie trucks in place of pony trucks, resulting in a 2-D-2 wheel arrangement and the electrics' reclassifications as S-motors.

In 1908 and 1909, New York Central ordered an additional 12 electrics, which were classed S-3, from General Electric.

Some of Central's S-motors served the Grand Central electrification until the early 1980s, outlasting the New York Central and its successor, Penn-Central. Several S-motors, including the pioneer, have been preserved, yet as of this writing in 2002 none have been properly restored for public display.

New York Central's Later Electrics

Between 1913 and 1926, General Electric built more advanced electric locomotives for New York Central. Classified as T-motors, they should not be confused with the

original T description. The Central listed 36 Class Ts in five subclasses that reflected slight variations on the design. All T-motors used an end-cab articulated design with an articulated B-B+B-B wheel arrangement, in which all wheels were powered. This allowed for a significantly more powerful locomotive with the full weight of the machine placed on the driving wheels, yet a lighter axle load as the weight was distributed more equally. According to *Jane's World Railways*, the T-2a motors weighed 280,500 pounds, all of which was available for traction, and produced 69,775 pounds starting tractive effort with a continuous tractive effort rating of 12,500 pounds at 57 miles per hour. Eight 330-horsepower gearless traction motors, one on each axle, produced 2,640 horsepower at 48 miles per hour, according to Hollingsworth. By comparison, New York Central information indicates that S-3 motors weighed 249,800 pounds, with 152,300 pounds available for adhesion. The S-3s produced just 38,075 pounds starting tractive effort and 4,870 pounds continuous tractive effort at 61 miles per hour. (Sources vary on the weight and tractive effort produced by these electrics, making accurate comparisons difficult.)

The articulated arrangement and smaller, lighter traction motors meant that the T-motors were much less damaging to tracks, and their superior performance earned them

the end-cab Class R. Central also ordered a fleet of R-1 electrics for its Detroit River Tunnel electrification that was undertaken following the success of Grand Central's electric operations. Like the New York electrification, this operation used a direct current (DC) underrunning third-rail. The R-1s were built in three subclasses, some of which were manufactured jointly by General Electric and Alco, while GE, in a pattern that seems to have been common for many years, solely built others.

Significant to the study of modern locomotives were big electrics using a 2-C+C-2 wheel arrangement built by GE in 1928 for the Central's Cleveland Union Terminal electrification, and 42 six-motor R-2s built in 1930 for Central's West Side operations. Both types used state-of-art, nose-suspended traction motors made possible by recent advances in motor technology. These powerful motors had made most earlier methods of DC motor-transmission designs obsolete. Although nose-suspended motors had been used since the 1890s on lightweight electric streetcars and small locomotives, until the 1920s these motors were not sufficiently

the majority of road passenger assignments and relegated the S-motors to secondary services.

New York Central later gave GE an order for seven Class Q motors that used steeple-cab design with a B-B wheel arrangement. Another type of B-B locomotive was

powerful for heavy traction applications. The power-to-weight ratio of a nose-suspended motor using older technology would have resulted in a motor too large and heavy for practical application, as the weight of such motors would have raised axle weights above acceptable limits. Other types of motors used more complicated types of motor transmission, such as the quill drives used on early electrics like the S-motors. Today, nose-suspended motors are standard equipment on diesel-electrics.

New York Central's R-2 electrics are of special interest to modern locomotive study not just because of their nose-suspended motors, but because they employed a C-C wheel arrangement (a pair of three-axle, three-motor, powered trucks). This same wheel and motor arrangement has subsequently become predominant on American road diesels today. The Central's pioneering use of the C-C arrangement predated its regular use on American lines by nearly three decades. In actual service, the Central's R-2 electrics were relatively obscure types primarily used on freight services on the route on the West Side of Manhattan, and thus were often relegated to nocturnal operation. In later years, a few R-2s were assigned to the Central's Detroit River Tunnel

electrified line, and in the late 1950s, the Chicago-area interurban Chicago, South Shore & South Bend acquired some former R-2s for freight services on its 1,500-volt DC overhead electric lines. The Cleveland Union Terminal electrics were originally designated P-1a. After the Cleveland Union Terminal overhead electrification was discontinued in favor of dieselization, the P-motors were rebuilt (receiving new subclasses P-2a and P2b) for third-rail operation on the Grand Central electrified lines.

More Electrification and More Electrics

In the first decades of the twentieth century considerable interest developed in electric operations, yet there was still disagreement as to what forms electric operations should take. The primary types of electrical systems were direct current, single-phase alternating current (AC), and three-phase AC. Several different electrification schemes developed, based on these basic types, and there were few established standards even among common types of electrification. The basic electrification configurations that emerged were low-voltage DC, transmitted via third-rail (as with the New York Central) or by overhead trolley wire (as used by street

Pennsylvania Railroad GG1 No. 4802 electric sits under wire at Ivy City Engine Terminal at Washington, D.C. This was one of 14 GG1s built for PRR by General Electric at Erie, Pennsylvania. In addition to these, GE supplied electrical components for many other GG1s. Although largely a PRR design, several firms undertook the construction of the 139-unit GG1 fleet. *Jim Shaughnessy*

Pennsylvania Railroad GG1 No. 4924 leads a westbound train on the High Line in the New Jersey Meadows near the west portal of the Penn Tunnels below the Hudson River. This GG1 was built by the railroad at its Altoona, Pennsylvania, shops using GE electrical components. *Richard Jay Solomon*

railways); moderate-voltage DC (usually between 1,500 and 3,000 volts), transmitted by overhead wire; high-voltage, single-phase AC (typically 11,000 volts in the United States); and three-phase AC (discussed in greater detail later).

As the New York Central was undertaking its third-rail DC electrification of Grand Central, New Haven Railroad worked with Westinghouse to pioneer high-voltage AC overhead for its suburban New York City lines. Since New Haven's trains accessed Grand Central via the New York Central, they also had to be able to operate off the Central's

DC third-rail. Pennsylvania Railroad also electrified its New York terminal operations, which included newly bored long tunnels under New York's Hudson and East Rivers. The Pennsy also electrified its extensive suburban operations on its Long Island Rail Road subsidiary, using a third-rail system similar to the New York Central's. The Pennsy chose Westinghouse as its supplier, and used an overrunning third-rail instead of the underrunning variety employed by New York Central. The greater efficiency of high-voltage AC transmission over long distances made this system more attractive for large-scale mainline electrification. Although the Pennsylvania had committed to DC third-rail for its New York terminal operations, it later adopted a high-voltage overhead system similar to the New Haven's for its Philadelphia suburban services. In the 1920s and 1930s, PRR expanded its overhead system for its Northeast Corridor electrification project between New York, Philadelphia, and Washington, D.C., and eventually to Harrisburg.

High-voltage AC projects were largely the domain of Westinghouse. By contrast, General Electric continued to develop and promote its own systems through the 1920s. While GE primarily built DC systems ranging from 600-volt electric trolley networks to extensive 3,000-volt systems, one of the most unusual projects the company undertook was the electrification of the Great Northern's Cascade Tunnel in 1911, using a three-phase AC system. Three-phase AC motors offer superior traction characteristics to DC motors, making them especially desirable for use on heavily graded lines. The difficulty in controlling three-phase AC motors, however, precluded wide-scale adoption of the system. Great Northern's electrics worked at 6,600 volts and required two separate sets of delivery wires. To haul GN trains, General Electric built a small fleet of boxcab electrics, each of which was rated at 1,500 horsepower, using four induction motors. The locomotives drew current using a pair of trolley poles, one pole for each set of wires. Great Northern's novel electrification was converted to a more conventional single-phase 11,000-volt AC system in the late 1920s, when the railroad relocated its Cascade crossing, which included a new and much longer Cascade Tunnel of 9.1 miles in length.

General Electric introduced higher-voltage DC electrification on interurban and suburban railway systems, such as Southern Pacific's Oakland, California, electrification. The

There should be little doubt as to the manufacturer of New York Central P-2b No. 235, seen here on April 13, 1957, with the *Empire State Express* at Grand Central Terminal in New York. General Electric rebuilt this former Cleveland Union Station electric in 1955 for New York third-rail service. In its modified form, it weighed 388,000 pounds and used six GE-755A traction motors.
Jim Shaughnessy

New Haven EP-5 No. 375 (left) and an EMD-built FL9 diesel-electric/electric are seen at the New Haven, Connecticut, engine terminal. The EP-5s were the first locomotives to wear New Haven's new "McGinnis" livery. Drawings of the EP-5 when the model was ordered show the type wearing the older green-and-gold scheme, such as that used on New Haven EP-4s.
Jim Shaughnessy

success with a 2,400-volt DC electrification on Montana's Butte, Anaconda & Pacific Railroad, the Milwaukee Road was keen to take advantage of cost savings afforded by electrified operations, and the railroad contracted with GE to supply it with 3,000-volt DC overhead electrification.

The Milwaukee's Rocky Mountain electrification stretched 440 miles from Harlowton, Montana, to Avery, Idaho, a small, isolated village located deep in the Bitterroot Mountains. Milwaukee's Cascade Mountain electrification ran from Othello, Washington, over the mountains to Tacoma and eventually on to Seattle.

Milwaukee's electrification, which began in 1915 and reached its fullest extent by 1927, was developed to satisfy different criteria than early eastern electrification programs. The Milwaukee Road used electrification to lower mainline operating costs on the Pacific Extension, where the railroad faced an unusual combination of circumstances. As one of the last transcontinental mainlines, the Milwaukee Road's route was completed in 1909, 40 years after the first transcontinental railroad. Operations were very difficult and faced steep and prolonged grades in the Rockies, Bitterroots, and Cascades of Montana, Idaho, and Washington. Where other western lines had supplies of coal or used oil-burning steam locomotives, Milwaukee's remote operations were

Milwaukee Road displayed one of its freshly shopped Bi-Polar electrics in Milwaukee, Wisconsin. One of these locomotives is now preserved in St. Louis, Missouri. Richard Jay Solomon collection, photographer unknown

foremost example of GE's high-voltage DC system, however, was the electrification of the Milwaukee Road's fabled Pacific Extension, a route that ultimately consisted of more than 660 route miles of electric operation and involved two long but noncontiguous sections of electrification. Inspired by GE's

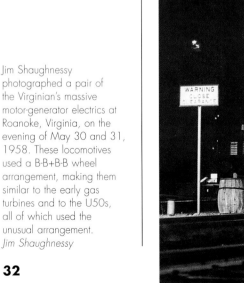

Jim Shaughnessy photographed a pair of the Virginian's massive motor-generator electrics at Roanoke, Virginia, on the evening of May 30 and 31, 1958. These locomotives used a B-B+B-B wheel arrangement, making them similar to the early gas turbines and to the U50s, all of which used the unusual arrangement. Jim Shaughnessy

Milwaukee's Bi-Polar Electrics

hampered by a lack of available fuel, and it needed to haul coal for hundreds of miles to supply its steam locomotives. Electric operations solved Milwaukee's fuel problems, as it harnessed hydroelectric power to provide electricity and more efficient propulsion. Another benefit was the ability of electric motors to develop very high starting tractive effort, useful in ascending the railroad's grades, some of which reached 2.2 percent. Through electrification, the Milwaukee Road minimized the use of helpers and operated longer, heavier freight trains over the mountains. Another cost saving was the pioneering use of regenerative braking, a feature that turned traction motors into electric generators that fed current back into the system when descending grades. This saved electricity costs and reduced brake-shoe wear.

GE and Alco jointly built two varieties of locomotives for Milwaukee's electric operations that appeared quite different externally. The freight locomotives were semi-permanently coupled pairs of Class EF-1 boxcabs built in 1915. These used a 2-B-B+B-B-2 arrangement, measured 112 feet long, and weighed 576,000 pounds, placing 451,000 pounds on the driving wheels. Using eight GE motors, one powering each driving axle, the boxcabs could produce 112,750 pounds tractive effort. (In his book, *The History of the Electric Locomotive*, F.J.G. Haut indicates a higher figure of 135,000 pounds of starting tractive effort and continuous output rated at 3,000 horsepower with a one-hour output at 3,440 horsepower.) These boxcabs were used on both electrified sections. Similar machines, designated EP-1, were

The year is 1938, and GE's Building 10 at Erie, Pennsylvania, is filled with New Haven EP-4 streamlined passenger electrics under construction. Over the decades, GE has built thousands of locomotives in this very same building, from GG1s and gas turbines to the latest AC6000CWs. *Smithsonian Institution Neg. No. 34206, William D. Middleton collection*

33

Milwaukee Road's electrification was discontinued in 1974, and most of the Pacific Extension west of South Dakota was abandoned in 1980. In this night scene, one of Milwaukee's "Little Joe" electrics rolls past vintage boxcab electric No. E-47A. Some of the original 42 boxcabs built by GE in 1915 and 1916 survived right until the end of the electrification. One is preserved in Duluth, Minnesota. *Mel Patrick*

initially used for passenger services on the Rocky Mountain electrified section.

In 1919, GE and Alco built five massive, three-piece articulated EP-2 electrics that used an unusual 1-B-D+D-B-1 arrangement, indicating the machines rode on 28 wheels, of which 24 were powered. They used a peculiar-looking center-cab configuration with elongated wagon-top hood-end sections that were slightly lower than the cab section. The entire machine was articulated, with the cab split in three sections. Enormous headlights rode on the top of the end hoods, and a General Electric Type 100 gearless bi-polar motor powered each of the 12 driving axles. As a result, the EP-2s were commonly known as the *Bi-Polars*. Maximum tractive effort figures vary, with some sources indicating 114,450 pounds. Haut indicates a higher figure of 137,340 pounds. Drawing 888 amps, the Bi-Polars could deliver 42,000 pounds of continuous tractive effort at 28.4 miles per hour and produce 3,200 horsepower for traction. (One hour of output was about 10 percent higher.) Today we might not be impressed by a single locomotive with a 3,200-horsepower output—GE's most powerful modern diesels can produce nearly double that figure—but in 1919, the Bi-Polars were real monsters. To demonstrate their

great power, Milwaukee staged a well-publicized tug of war in the Cascades between a single Bi-Polar electric and two steam locomotives, a 2-6-6-2 Mallet compound and a conventional 2-8-0 Consolidation. In a show of brute force, the electric dragged the working steam locomotives across the bridge. In daily service, the Bi-Polars were intended to lift a 1,000-ton transcontinental passenger train up a 2 percent grade at a steady 25 miles per hour.

At the time, the Milwaukee Road's great mountain electrification was viewed as a triumph for modern technology. Proponents of electrification hoped that the Milwaukee's electrification would set an example that other lines would follow. It even inspired a work of fiction, *Tom Swift and His Electric Locomotive*. But while Milwaukee's electrification offered operational benefits, it remained an anomaly in American operating practice and was not repeated on such a scale; high-voltage AC ultimately prevailed over GE's DC system for use on heavy overhead electrification. However, electrification, which seemed to be the power of the future in 1920, never caught on in America. While more lines were electrified, the percentage of electrified mainline remained very small. The situation was different overseas, where a different economy prevailed. In Europe, not only did electrification become the dominant form of railway power, several countries adopted the 3,000-volt DC standard, including Belgium, Italy, and Poland. Perhaps the most extensive use of DC electric traction is in the former Soviet Union.

Oddly enough, Russian railways influenced Milwaukee's last electric motive power acquisition. In 1947 and 1948, General Electric was building a fleet of 20 massive double-ended streamlined 2-D+D-2 electrics for the Soviet electrified railways when Cold War politics intervened to prevent their delivery. With American-Soviet relations tenuous at best, GE sought other buyers for the orphaned machines. With its extensive 3,000-volt electrification, the Milwaukee Road was an obvious sales candidate, so GE lent the railroad a locomotive for testing. Because the locomotives were designed for Russian gauge—which, thanks to American engineer George Washington Whistler, had been established 100 years earlier as 5 feet instead of the 4 feet, 8-1/2 inches used in the United States—the big machine needed to be re-gauged for operation on the Milwaukee. The locomotives earned the nickname "Little Joes" after Soviet dictator Joseph Stalin. The

Milwaukee Road bought 12 Little Joes in 1950 for its Rocky Mountain lines, while Indiana interurban South Shore picked up three. The remaining five were sold to the Paulista Railway in Brazil.

More AC Electrics

By 1930, high-voltage, single-phase AC transmission systems had become the predominant choice for electrification. The New Haven, Pennsylvania, Boston & Maine, Virginian, and Norfolk & Western railroads, among others, all adopted 11,000-volt AC systems. General Electric built a variety of single-phase AC machines for various lines. In the 1930s and early 1940s, it built several classes of electrics for the New Haven, including 10 EP-3 articulated boxcabs in 1931. These were designed for 70-mile-per-hour passenger service; they used the 2-C+C-2 wheel arrangement developed a

Pennsylvania Railroad E44 electrics lead an eastbound in the Pennsylvania Dutch country east of Lancaster. General Electric's E44s were the railroad's last new electrics. *Richard Jay Solomon*

few years earlier for the Cleveland Union Terminal electrics. New Haven's EP-3s were 77 feet long with a 66-foot wheelbase. They used six twin-arm, 12-pole motors, one for each powered axle, using a quill-and-cup drive, providing a continuous 2,740 horsepower with a 3,440-horsepower one-hour rating (in AC territory). When operating on DC third-rail trackage to reach Grand Central Terminal, motor output was slightly lower. The type delivered 68,400 pounds of starting tractive effort. The EP-3's high output and excellent tracking qualities at higher speeds led the Pennsylvania Railroad to borrow one for testing in 1934 when it was trying to develop a better electric for its Northeast Corridor operations. Experiments with the EP-3 led the PRR to adopt the 2-C+C-2 wheel arrangement for its very successful high-output, high-speed streamlined GG1 electric. Several manufacturers, including GE, over a nine-year period beginning in 1934, built the Pennsy's GG1 fleet. General Electric also provided electrical equipment for

GG1s built by PRR at Altoona, as well as by Baldwin. The railroad divided the supply of electric gear for its electric fleet between GE and Westinghouse.

In 1938, the New Haven placed a repeat order with GE for six EP-4 electrics based on the EP-3 design. The EP-4s were similar to the EP-3s in most respects but featured a handsome double-ended streamlined carbody and were slightly more powerful. They were given a 3,600-horsepower continuous output rating and designed to operate up to 93 miles per hour. In 1943, Alco-GE and Baldwin-Westinghouse evenly split an order for 10 similar streamlined EF-3 electrics designed for freight service. These were numbered in the 0150 series and strictly intended for AC overhead operation. As a result, they were not equipped with third-rail shoes and could not run into Grand Central. The EF-3s used a lower gearing and developed 90,000 pounds starting tractive effort while producing 4,860 horsepower at their maximum speed of 65 miles per hour.

Although the American market for electric locomotives has not amounted to much since the end of World War II, General Electric has sold numerous electrics for export. On February 24, 1978, the Taiwan Railway Administration opened its electrification with GE electric E42 No. 201 and a 15-car special train. *William D. Middleton*

慶祝鐵路電化一期工程工竣通車

On February 21, 1976, five weeks before bankrupt Penn-Central would become the primary component of Conrail, a pair of former Pennsylvania Railroad E44s leads a freight at Harrisburg, Pennsylvania. Electrified freight railroading did not fit into Conrail's operating scheme, and a few years after this photo was made, Conrail's electric operations were discontinued.
Doug Eisele

AC-DC Converter Locomotives

In the early years, AC-electrified lines employed motor-generator locomotives that reduced line current to a lower voltage for use by single-phase AC-traction motors. By the mid-1920s, advances in technology resulted in the construction of hybrid locomotives that converted single-phase AC power to DC power, which allowed high-voltage AC locomotives to use DC-traction motors that were better suited for railway traction. Between 1926 and 1930, both Baldwin-Westinghouse and Alco-GE built several classes of AC-DC motor-generator locomotives for the Great Northern Railway. The most impressive GN electrics were two massive streamliners constructed by Alco-GE in 1946 that measured 101 feet long and weighed 735,000 pounds. They employed a B-D+D-B wheel arrangement in which all axles were powered. Transformers converted line voltage from 11,000 volts AC to 1,350 volts AC. This current was used to turn a pair of DC generators, which, in turn, fed power to 12 General Electric 746 nose-suspended traction motors, one powering each axle. Using a 17:70 gear ratio, these electrics developed 183,750 pounds starting tractive effort and 119,000 pounds continuous tractive effort at just over 15 miles per hour; they were rated at 5,000 horsepower. The Great Northern's electrics were followed two years later by two pairs of streamlined AC-DC motor-generator electrics for the Virginian; each pair used a B-B-B-B+B-B-B-B wheel arrangement with GE 752 traction motors.

By the 1950s, advances in mercury-arc technology made for the development of high-voltage AC-DC rectifiers that superseded motor-generator technology. New Haven was among the first lines to use rectifier electric locomotives. After first employing the technology in a fleet of passenger electric multiple-unit cars, New Haven ordered 10 EP-5 streamlined passenger electric locomotives from GE that used Ignitron rectifier tubes. These machines rode on C-C swing-bolster trucks and nose-suspended traction motors similar to those used by modern diesel-electrics. The EP-5s were 68 feet long, weighed 348,000 pounds, and produced 87,000 pounds maximum tractive effort. They featured the modern, new McGinnis livery using swatches of white, black, and orange, replacing New Haven's more traditional dark green–and-gold scheme.

Virginian ordered one dozen Ignitron rectifiers from GE in 1955 for coal service. Delivered over the next two years, they were among the first electrics to use a road-switcher configuration. They rode on C-C trucks and produced 3,300 horsepower. The Virginian's electrification was discontinued after the company was bought by Norfolk & Western in 1960. New Haven bought the 12 Ignitron electrics in 1963, repainted them, and reclassified them as EF-4s for freight service between New York City and New Haven, Connecticut.

The Pennsylvania Railroad followed Virginian's example and ordered a fleet of Ignitron rectifier electrics using the C-C road switcher configuration. Designated E44 (electric, 4,400 horsepower), they were intended to replace the PRR's aging fleet of 1930s-era boxcabs in freight service. While the E44 was in production, advances in silicon diode technology superseded the use of water-cooled Ignitron rectifier tubes. The later E44s were built as silicon-diode rectifiers, while earlier machines were later retrofitted with the updated technology. A total of 66 E44s were built, with the first delivered in 1960.

Diesel-Electric vs. Straight Electric

For decades, American railroads eyed electrification cautiously, carefully weighing the advantages of straight-electric operations against the high costs of electrifying their lines.

In his book, *From Bullets to BART*, William D. Middleton points out that "in 1938, America led the world in railroad electrification." Yet, from that point onward, very little new mainline electrification was undertaken in the United States. Following World War II, American railroads favored large-scale dieselization, and in the two decades from 1940 to 1960, railroads rapidly dispensed with their steam locomotive fleets in favor of new diesels. During this steam-diesel transition period, many railroads that had experimented with electrification discontinued their electric operations. Since many early railroad electrifications were implemented to avoid the negative effects of steam locomotive smoke, the use of diesels had most the advantages of electrification while providing greater operational flexibility. Railroads found little cost incentive to maintain separate fleets of electric locomotives.

Short-term economics was a dominant consideration in switching from steam power to another power source, and American railroads found it difficult to justify the much greater initial expense of electric operations over dieselization. To offset high costs, the Pennsylvania Railroad's 1930s electrification had benefited from government loans.

In Europe, the situation was different. European railways were generally state-run institutions and viewed by their respective governments as strategic national infrastructure. As a result, railways enjoyed the benefits of long-term strategic planning and large subsidies and investment. Following World War II, European countries invested heavily in railway infrastructure, while the U.S. government focused on a nationally subsidized highway infrastructure. European railways embraced large-scale electrification for a variety of reasons: The high costs of electrification were less of a concern there because the cost could be financed by government sources. Also, European railways were not taxed on capital improvements, as were America's private railroads. In addition, most European countries rely more heavily on imported fuels, with significantly higher costs than in the United States. Electrification allowed countries without substantial oil reserves to take advantage of another form of power.

By the early 1980s, remaining mainline electrified operations in the United States were almost exclusively for passenger services. The Milwaukee Road discontinued its last electric operations in 1974, and Conrail, which had

assumed operation of freight services on former Pennsylvania Railroad and New Haven lines, discontinued electric operations by 1981. One example of new electrification occurred in the late 1990s, when Amtrak electrified its Northeast Corridor line from New Haven to Boston in preparation for its new *Acela Express* high-speed passenger services.

Massive investment in the electrification of European railways, meanwhile, spurred greater levels of research and development in European electric locomotive designs and gave companies such as ASEA, Alstom, and Siemens direct access to substantial markets for new electrics. So, advanced electric locomotive designs became the domain of European, as well as Japanese, builders. While General Electric continued to offer electric locomotives through the 1970s and 1980s, the lack of demand and more advanced

European designs resulted in only a handful of GE electrics for domestic services. GE has, however, sold numerous electrics for export to a variety of nations.

Today, the American market for electrics is dominated by European designs that are usually manufactured domestically under contract.

E60 Electrics

In the early 1970s, Amtrak needed new electrics to replace the aging former Pennsylvania Railroad GG1 fleet. Amtrak, of course, had acquired the fleet when the federal government created the national passenger company to relieve ailing freight railroads of revenue-losing passenger services. To meet these requirements, GE built a fleet of 26 double-ended, high-horsepower E60CP/E60CH electrics for

high-speed passenger services. According to *The Contemporary Diesel Spotter's Guide* by Louis Marre and Jerry Pinkepank, the E60CP contained a steam generator to provide heat and lighting for traditional passenger equipment; the E60CHs were equipped with the more modern head-end electric power for heat and electricity.

Amtrak's locomotives were based on a single-ended E60C type built for the Black Mesa & Lake Powell line in Arizona. The E60 types use a cowl design, in which the outer body is not integral to the structure of the locomotive. Amtrak's E60CP/E60CHs were unadorned, flat-fronted machines dressed in its red-blue-and-silver scheme. These Spartan-looking utilitarian machines produced 6,000 horsepower output and delivered 75,000 pounds starting tractive effort. Although intended for 120-mile-per-hour service, Amtrak's E60CP/E60CH locomotives suffered from a

flawed truck design and were later relegated to a maximum speed of 85 miles per hour.

As a result, Amtrak sought a more effective high-speed locomotive and ultimately settled on a derivative of the highly successful Swedish Rc4 type, designated AEM-7, and built under license by EMD. Following the arrival the AEM-7s in the early 1980s, Amtrak sold some of its E60s to New Jersey Transit, a suburban passenger operator, and the Navajo Mine, a mining railway in New Mexico. However, some were retained by Amtrak and remain in regular passenger service. In later years, Amtrak E60s were frequently used on heavy long-distance trains that traverse the Northeast Corridor between New York and Washington, D.C. In the early 1980s, GE built a pair of E60C-2s for the Deseret Western, a 35-mile-long coal railway operating in Colorado and Utah, as well as similar types for export.

General Electric built 26 double-ended, high-horsepower E60CP/E60CH electrics for Amtrak in 1974 and 1975. In later years they were often assigned to heavy trains, such as through New York–Florida runs. Amtrak E60CP No. 607 leads a 16-car *Silver Star* through Newark, Delaware, on Election Day, November 3, 1992. *Brian Solomon*

EARLY DIESELS, ALCO-GE, AND SWITCHERS

General Electric was instrumental in the early development of internal-combustion motive power and electrical transmission for railway applications. Perhaps no other company in the world contributed as much basic research and development during the formative era of diesel-electric development. General Electric was one of the first to experiment with gas-electric railcars, internal-combustion locomotives, and the first to experiment with, build, and sell diesel locomotives. Much of GE's early work contributed directly to the development of its later locomotive designs, as well of those of its competitors.

By 1904, General Electric was a leader in electric traction systems. Its work with electric streetcar and electric interurban systems was well established, and it was a preferred supplier for emergent heavy-railroad electrification systems. A logical extension of this business was the development of self-powered electrical railway motive power. GE was not the first to experiment with gas-electrics; William Patton had built a gasoline-electric-powered railcar using a small 10-horsepower Van Duzen engine in 1890, believed to be the first such application of this technology on a railway vehicle. Patton later built more gasoline-electric railcars, but ended production in 1893. He is also credited with building a few gasoline-electric locomotives, but these did not function well and his ideas did not have an immediate effect on the development of more effective technology. A few years later, the self-propelled gas-electric car gained interest in England.

General Electric had followed these developments and in 1904 initiated its own gas-electric experiments. (This was the same year that GE built the New York Central's prototype electric locomotive for the Grand Central Terminal electrification.) GE used a wooden Barney & Smith combine-coach provided by the Delaware & Hudson and a Wolseley gasoline engine from England. Based on these early trials, GE developed its own gasoline engine line and became one of the largest early manufacturers of gas-electric railcars—lightweight, self-propelled passenger cars commonly known as *Doodlebugs*. These cars used bodies manufactured by the Wason Car Manufacturing Company of Springfield, Massachusetts, and were very similar to the types of cars used by electric street railways. GE sold its first gas-electric cars in 1906 and built approximately 89 of them through 1917. Most of GE's cars were built prior to 1914, and only a few were built after that.

The production of gas-electric railcars led to GE's development of internal-combustion locomotives. Although today we may differentiate between *railcars* and *locomotives*, the development of these two types of machines is closely intertwined. In GE's case, both used internal-combustion engines for power with an electric-traction transmission. While this initial effort did not result in a commercial enterprise, it

A vintage General Electric herald. *Brian Solomon*

was part of the process that ultimately led GE into the diesel-electric locomotive business. (The company's earliest work with Rudolf Diesel's engine is described in the sidebar "The First Diesel" by John Gruber.)

General Electric engineers Henry Chatain and Hermann Lemp are credited with pioneering much of the company's early internal-combustion locomotive technology. Interestingly, both men were immigrants from Switzerland. According to Jerry A. Pinkepank in the November 1996 issue of *TRAINS Magazine*, Chatain designed GE's early gas engines, while Lemp was responsible for the development of electrical control systems. It is known that Chatain met with Rudolf Diesel and the men exchanged ideas. According to an article titled "A Brief History of Erie General Electric 1911–1994," published in *The Journal of Erie Studies* in the spring of 1995, GE in 1906 put Chatain in charge of its Gas Engine Department, which was relocated to Erie, Pennsylvania, in 1911. As a result, the Erie facility, rather than the one in Schenectady, developed as GE's primary locomotive works. In 1912 Chatain filed a patent with the U.S. Patent Office detailing improvements in the design of an internal combustion–electric locomotive. In it, Chatain articulated his idea in great detail:

> "In a locomotive, the combination of an engine, projections that extend downwardly from the engine base and form with the base the magnet frame of an electric motor, field coils carried by the projections, a truck, and armature for the motor that is mounted on an axle of the truck and is located between said projections, and a generator driven by the engine which is adapted to supply current to the motor."

While the precise arrangement described by Chatain may seem peculiar, the fundamentals of the modern diesel-electric are clearly outlined.

Dan Patch 100

Among GE's gas-electric railcar customers was the newly formed Minneapolis, St. Paul, Rochester & Dubuque Electric Traction Company, a lightly built interurban railway better known as the Dan Patch Line. While it was similar to many interurban lines operating all over the United

Although not the first diesel-electric locomotive, Central Railroad of New Jersey No. 1000 is generally considered the first successful commercial diesel-electric locomotive. It was built in 1925 by a consortium of General Electric, Alco, and Ingersoll-Rand. Today, old CNJ 1000 is proudly displayed at the Baltimore & Ohio Railroad Museum in Baltimore, Maryland. *Brian Solomon*

States, it differed from most "electric" railways in that it used gas-electric technology instead of overhead trolley wire or a third-rail for propulsion. To meet the needs of the Dan Patch Line, General Electric built a small boxcab gas-electric locomotive using a carbody constructed by the Wason Car Company. GE installed two of its 8x10-inch V-8 engines rated at 175 horsepower each. The locomotive was 36 feet, 4 inches long, weighed 57 tons, and rode on a pair of two-axle trucks giving it a B-B wheel arrangement—typical of interurban electric locomotives of the period. While not the very first gasoline-electric locomotive, Dan Patch No. 100 is generally considered the first commercially successful internal combustion–electric locomotive in the United States. GE built several more similar machines for the Dan Patch Line and other railways.

One of the difficulties with the early gas-electric cars and locomotives was effectively controlling engine output. For an internal combustion–electric engine to operate efficiently, output must match the load drawn by the traction motors—excess engine output wastes energy, and inadequate output can result in the locomotive stalling. In extreme situations, mismatched output and load can damage equipment and delay a train. Between 1916 and 1919, Hermann Lemp devised a control system for optimal performance by matching engine and traction characteristics and placing them under the direction of a single throttle handle. This pioneering work became the basis of most practical diesel locomotive control systems used by American manufacturers.

Commercial Diesel Development

In 1917, General Electric pioneered another technological development with the construction of an experimental diesel-electric locomotive based on its earlier gas-electric designs. The new locomotive used a GM50 engine, a V-8 designed by Chatain and similar to GE's gasoline engines. According to John Kirkland in *The Diesel Builders*, it employed concepts adopted from German Junkers engines designed for aircraft applications. It produced 225 horsepower, 50 more than GE's gasoline engine, and weighed almost 7 tons. GE built several diesel-electric locomotives based around this engine for commercial use in 1918. One was delivered to the Jay Street Connecting Railroad, where it

Continued on page 48

THE FIRST DIESEL By John Gruber

General Electric supplied the generator and electric parts for the first diesel-electric locomotive, built for Southern Pacific, in 1904 and 1905, while a GE founder provided the technical expertise for its development.

Dr. Rudolf Diesel, the engine's inventor, had been in the United States in May to promote a stationary engine displayed at the St. Louis World's Fair. St. Louis brewery magnate Augustus Busch, through the Diesel Motor Company of America and later the American Diesel Engine Company, controlled the U.S. patent rights for the engine Diesel had developed in Germany.

Word of the new locomotive appeared in *The New York Times* on October 2, 1904, as Busch returned from a five-month tour of Europe. Busch proclaimed that the oil-burning diesel engine was "the most economical stationary engine, in which capacity it is being used here as well as abroad in generating power for water works, electric lighting plants, and industries generally." He went on to reveal that the engine was presently "being applied to locomotives, a 200-ton internal-combustion locomotive having just been ordered by the Southern Pacific Railroad for a thorough trial."

After the *Manufacturers' Record* of Baltimore, Maryland, confirmed the details in its October 13, 1904, issue, newspapers around the country picked up the story. "New Locomotive Monster Coming," the *San Francisco Chronicle* headline said. "New Type of Locomotive To Do Wonders," added the *Chicago Tribune*.

The International Power Company, which had been making stationary diesel engines, coordinated the production of the new locomotive. Its president, Joseph H. Hoadley, applied for a patent for an "improved system of electric railways," using an internal-combustion engine and generator. Walter H. Knight, the General Electric founder and its first chief engineer, was chief engineer for International Power. The Corliss Works of Providence, Rhode Island, built the diesel engine, and American Locomotive Company of Schenectady, New York, built the trucks and frame.

Kyle Williams Wyatt, now a curator at the California State Railroad Museum in Sacramento, wrote about the SP diesel in *The Railway &*

Locomotive Historical Society Newsletter (Fall 1996), based on a two-page article in the *Marconigram* (December 1904). "The locomotive for which the Southern Pacific has contracted is of revolutionary design, and might be easily characterized as a powerhouse on wheels.... It uses no coal and therefore there are no ashes, sparks or cinders with the customary attendant nuisances," wrote J. Langford King in the New York City magazine. The *Marconigram*, *New York Press*, and *Chronicle* carried an identical illustration of the locomotive in November and December.

Wyatt also cited an item in the *Railway Master Mechanic* (April 1905): "The Southern Pacific company has been making a series of experiments with a motor car which is driven by electric motors at the axles, the current being furnished by dynamos, directly connected to large Diesel oil engines, located in the car."

John P. Hankey, a historian, provided an international context for the development in a talk at the Association of Railroad Museums in 2000. Even a century ago, American railroading was part of a global technological community. "The diesel-electric locomotive is based on a prime mover perfected by an eccentric German engineer (Rudolf Diesel), using the thermodynamic theory of a mid-nineteenth-century French mathematician (Sadi Canot)," Hankey stated. "The electrical gear was based on the dynamo invented by Thomas Edison, who relied on the work of an English physicist named James Clerk Maxwell.

"The control technology was made possible by a Serbian-born electrical engineer named Nicola Tesla, and it all basically started with an Italian named Alessandro Volta, who perfected the pile, or electric storage battery, about 1800. We won't even speak of steel technology perfected by the Germans, French, and English, or about petroleum refining, or the inventors of the machine tools used to make the locomotives."

Magazines, newspapers, and trade publications confirm the 1904 and 1905 dates. What happened during the tests is not known, but they must have been unsuccessful, since the locomotive dropped out of sight. Nevertheless, the story of its planning offers new insights into the development of diesel-electric locomotives in the United States.

Continued from page 46

Anti-pollution laws in cities created the market for diesel-electric switchers. The GE-Alco-IR consortium built a number of slow-speed 300-horsepower boxcabs for urban switching services. Reading Company No. 50 was nearly identical to Central Railroad of New Jersey No. 1000. *William D. Middleton collection*

was designated No. 4 and joined the earlier GE gas-electric, No. 3. Two others were built, one for the city of Baltimore and the other for the U.S. Army. None of the diesels performed well, and all had very brief careers. Shortly after they were built, GE decided to exit the business of designing and manufacturing internal-combustion engines.

For several years, General Electric's diesel-electric work lay mostly dormant. After World War I, the growth of highway-based transport started to seriously affect railroad revenue, as cars, buses, and trucks competed for railroad traffic. In the early 1920s, however, there was a resurgent demand for gas-electric railcars as North American railways sought measures to reduce the costs of operating lightly traveled branchline and rural passenger services. Although GE did

not redevelop its gas-electric railcar business, it became the dominant electrical supplier for the Electro-Motive Corporation, a new company led by Harold Hamilton that dominated the gas-electric railcar market in the 1920s. By mid-decade, General Electric had renewed its interest in diesel-electric technology. (In 1930, EMC was bought by General Motors and eventually developed into the foremost locomotive builder, Electro-Motive Division, or EMD.)

General Electric decided against further design of its own diesel engines and instead worked with established engine producer Ingersoll-Rand (IR). The two companies joined forces in 1923 and constructed an experimental diesel-electric locomotive using GE electrical and mechanical components and IR's successful 10x12-inch, six-cylinder diesel engine. This slow-speed engine operated at

550 rpm, about half the speed of today's 7FDL used in modern GEs, and generated just 300 horsepower. Designated No. 8835 (GE's construction number), this machine first moved under its own power at IR's Phillipsburg, Pennsylvania, plant on December 17, 1923. In June 1924, No. 8835 began a tour of eastern railways and was tested by 13 different companies, including Central Railroad of New Jersey.

Development of GE's diesel prototype coincided with the passing of New York City's Kaufman Act, legislation that expanded on earlier pollution laws and effectively banned the operation of steam locomotives within New York City by 1926. While most passenger operations had been electrified as a result of early laws, freight and switching operations in New York had remained steam powered. The worst offender was New York Central's heavily used West Side freight line in Manhattan. New York's other railroads were not afforded direct land access to the city and instead served New York via car float and barges that reached small isolated yards along the city's rivers and bays. It was not economical to electrify these small yards, and the diesel switcher allowed railroads to comply with the Kaufman Act without electrification. Amendments eventually postponed the Kaufman Act's strict 1926 deadline. Like the legislation that preceded it, however, the act forced railroads to seek alternative power, creating a market for GE's diesel-electric switchers.

The success of No. 8835 encouraged GE, Ingersoll-Rand, and the locomotive builder Alco to enter a business consortium to construct diesel-electric switching locomotives for commercial application. The arrangement was similar to the agreement that GE and Alco had enjoyed for two decades in the construction of straight electrics. Alco built mechanical components—frames, wheels, trucks, etc.; GE provided electrical components; and Ingersoll-Rand supplied the diesel engine and was also responsible for marketing. Between 1925 and 1928, the Alco-GE–Ingersoll-Rand consortium built 33 of the boxcab diesel-electrics, primarily for switching in eastern cities, especially New York City. Two models were offered: a 60-ton, 300-horsepower locomotive similar to demonstrator No. 8835, and a dual-engine, 100-ton locomotive that generated 600 horsepower.

In 1925, the Central Railroad of New Jersey took delivery of the first commercially built locomotive, one of the 300-horsepower boxcab variety that it designated No. 1000. This pioneering locomotive, today regarded as the first successful

diesel-electric built in the United States, was assigned to CNJ's isolated waterfront terminal in The Bronx. Unlike GE's earlier diesels, No. 1000 enjoyed a long and productive career, running for more than 30 years in the service it was built for. It was retired in 1957 and sent to the Baltimore & Ohio Railroad Museum in Baltimore for public display.

New York Central had the largest and most extensive freight operation in New York City. Although the railroad undertook the elevation and electrification of its West Side line in the late 1920s, it was not practical to electrify all of its branches and spurs. Furthermore, some of its spurs operated directly into warehouses in Manhattan, where even

During World War II and the immediate postwar dieselization, Alco and General Electric worked together in the production and marketing of diesel-electric locomotives. The new locomotives carried joint builders' plates. *Brian Solomon*

Among the types built jointly by Alco-GE were the RS-1 and RS-2/RS-3 road switchers. In this June 1961 photo made in Chicago, a Chicago & Western Indiana RS-1 leads a short passenger train, while Rock Island RS-3s (built in 1950 and 1951) idle between assignments. *Richard Jay Solomon*

General Electric's 44-ton model was specifically designed to weigh less than the 90,000 pounds maximum allowed for operations without a fireman under union work rules. The 44-tonner was popular with both shortlines and some Class I railroads for use on lightweight lines. On January 25, 1977, a pair of Aroostook Valley 44-tonners works at Washburn Junction, Maine. Locomotive No. 11 is a 380-horsepower model built in 1945, while No. 12 is a 400-horsepower model built in 1949. *Don Marson*

a diesel engine would produce unacceptable emissions. To solve Central's switching quandary, GE and Alco developed a tri-power locomotive that could operate as a straight third-rail electric, as a battery-powered electric, or as a battery-electric/diesel-electric drawing power from batteries while being charged by the onboard diesel engine. (The diesel engine would charge the batteries, but the third-rail connection could not.) After testing a center-cab tri-power prototype in February 1928, New York Central ordered a fleet of the locomotives using a more typical boxcab configuration. Most tri-power locomotives worked in the New York terminal area, although some were assigned to Chicago, Detroit, and Boston. Another locomotive, built to New York Central's specs, was delivered to the Rock Island for switching at LaSalle Street Station in Chicago. Alco left the consortium in 1928 to pursue its own diesel manufacturing business, while GE and Ingersoll-Rand continued to manufacture diesels together until the mid-1930s.

In 1934, the Electro-Motive Corporation—by this time owned by General Motors—stunned the railroad world with flashy, high-speed diesel streamlined trains. Sleek streamliners were an outgrowth of EMC's railcar business, which combined new automotive manufacturing techniques with recently developed compact, high-horsepower diesel engines.

General Electric had provided EMC with electrical gear during that company's formative years as a diesel-electric producer. Although diesel-electric streamliners captured the public spotlight during the mid-1930s, the largest segment of the diesel locomotive market was actually for new switchers. General Electric continued to focus its own diesel production on freight diesels and left the production and design of streamlined trains to other manufacturers. GE employed a variety of different diesel engines, including those manufactured by Busch-Sulzer, Caterpillar, Cooper-Bessemer, and Cummins. Its locomotives varied from relatively small switchers to the largest and most powerful diesel-electrics constructed up to that time.

In 1936, GE built two heavy six-motor diesels for Illinois Central, powerful machines designed for slow-speed transfer service in the Chicago area. Illinois Central No. 9200 was an 1,800-horsepower machine powered by a pair of Ingersoll-Rand six-cylinder engines, while IC No. 9201 was rated at 2,000 horsepower and powered by a 10-cylinder Busch-Sulzer diesel. According to Louis Marre in *Diesel Locomotives: The First 50 Years*, the latter locomotive was the most powerful single-engine diesel in the United States until the Alco-GE PA passenger locomotive was introduced a decade later.

Alco-GE

In the mid- to late 1930s, the locomotive industry was in flux. Some railroads remained firmly committed to traditional steam power, others considered large-scale electrification, and still others watched the development of new and more powerful diesel-electrics with close interest. (During this time, the Pennsylvania Railroad was enjoying the benefits of having electrified its New York–Washington lines.) The development of new steam types and unusual motive power, such as GE's steam turbine–electric, made uncertain the future of railroad locomotion. General Electric, however, was in a pretty comfortable position in the railroad industry, as the primary supplier of electric traction systems and electric locomotives, and as an established builder of diesel-electric switchers.

By the late 1930s, Electro-Motive had emerged as the leading producer of diesel-electric locomotives. EMC had introduced its E-unit line of passenger locomotives and developed its new and more reliable 567 series two-cycle diesel to replace the troubled Winton 201A engine used in its earliest locomotives. In 1938, EMC began manufacturing its own electrical components, basing its designs largely on GE's. As a result, GE no longer had EMC as a customer. Then in 1939, EMC debuted its four-unit FT road freight diesel, a machine that would convince many railroads that full-scale dieselization was both practical and affordable. While steam manufacturers believed they could hold on to a portion of the market for a few more years, many in the industry realized that the total dieselization of American railroads would soon be under way.

In 1940, Alco and GE combined forces to counter the diesel-producing power of EMC, soon to be reorganized as EMD, the Electro-Motive Division of General Motors. The two companies entered an agreement for the production and marketing of diesel-electric locomotives and worked together in the design of locomotives. Both manufacturers were listed on builders' plates, promotional literature, and advertising. Although General Electric's most notable contributions remained locomotive electrical systems, it also contributed to the industrial design of some postwar locomotives. (See the sidebar "GE Industrial Design" by John Gruber.)

In the 1930s, Alco had developed a successful line of heavy switchers powered by McIntosh & Seymore 531 series diesels. Alco expanded upon this engine design and by 1940 had upgraded to its 539 engine line, which was used to power its 600- and 1,000-horsepower S-model switchers. Both models used a six-cylinder diesel, but the 1,000-horsepower units used a turbocharged variety to obtain the higher horsepower rating. These switchers, like Alco's earlier models, used an end-cab design.

In 1941, at the request of the Rock Island, Alco expanded its switcher line to include a road-switcher type, the

first of its kind. Rock Island had desired a branchline loco-motive capable of a variety of tasks with the intent of reduc-ing branchline expenses by eliminating steam locomotives. Alco's RS-1 (a designation assigned to the type many years after the first locomotive was actually built) was basically a 1,000-horsepower switcher on a longer frame that allowed for a short hood that could house a boiler for steam heat. Many authorities concur that the RS-1 was the first true diesel-electric road switcher, a locomotive type that became predominant from the late 1950s onward. The RS-1 was de-veloped immediately prior to the United States' involvement in World War II, and the U.S. Army found the new loco-motive especially well suited to military applications. Consequently, it ordered several for work overseas. Many of these locomotives used six-axle trucks rather than the

four-axle trucks applied to civilian locomotives. Alco also built an export model of the RS-1 that used A1A trucks to reduce axle loadings and allow the type to work on lightly built track.

Beginning in 1940, Alco offered a streamlined road diesel designed for either high-speed passenger service or road freight work. These locomotives were known by their specification numbers, DL-103 to DL-110, and featured dis-tinctive styling by noted industrial designer Otto Kuhler. A pair of turbocharged 538 or 539 series diesels powered them, and most were used exclusively in passenger service. The largest fleet comprised 60 DL-109s built for New Haven.

The advent of World War II had profound implications for the development and production of diesel-electric loco-motives. In April 1942, the War Production Board (WPB),

A U.S. Navy Public Works GE center-cab switcher works a Chesapeake & Ohio car float ferry at the Norfolk, Virginia, Naval Base in 1963. General Electric built more than 1,100 switchers for use by the U.S. military and for dock companies. *William D. Middleton*

GE INDUSTRIAL DESIGN By John Gruber

Raymond E. Patten (1897–1948) helped shape the distinctive appearance of Alco and General Electric locomotives. Among his best-known railroad designs were the Alco-GE PA (passenger) and FA (freight) diesel locomotives in 1946. Patten, director of GE's Appearance Design Division of the Appliance and Merchandising Department in Bridgeport, Connecticut, also influenced the designs of electric and industrial locomotives and the ill-fated Union Pacific steam turbine–electric.

Design patents applied for in 1946 and granted in 1949 confirm Patten's role in the PA/FA models. From 1940 to 1953, Alco and GE jointly marketed large road locomotives and distributed a six-page article that Patten prepared. The goal, he said, was "A locomotive so distinctive and so powerful looking that it actually helps the railroads sell their services to passengers and shippers."

From rough pencil sketches of the exterior, executives selected the basic design. The fluted headlight, "devised to obtain product identity and serve as a focal point," had to be changed to meet Interstate Commerce Commission (ICC) regulations. The modifications throughout the design process are reflected in the advertising. Melbourne Brindle's painting for the August 1946 GE calendar and other early illustrations, for example, show the headlight grille before it was moved higher on the nose. *TRAINS Magazine* in September 1946 also featured an early version of the PA.

Patten attended Massachusetts Institute of Technology, started his career with the Hume Body Corporation of Boston, and continued custom body designs with the Dayton Wright Company. He spent five years with the Packard Motor Car Commune of Detroit and joined the Edison GE Company in Chicago in 1928. When he moved to Bridgeport in 1934, he was the only person in the appliance design department. Under his leadership, the department grew to 50 by 1946, broadening its tasks to include packaging and the design of dealer stores.

Patten won a $1,000 award in 1940 for "an electric range as sightly as a grand piano," according to an announcement in *The New York Times*. In the same competition, Henry Dreyfuss, who streamlined the *20th Century Limited*, received an award for "a washing machine elegant enough for a drawing room." Patten's contacts with the GE builders were mostly through the mail and purchase orders. He made airbrush renderings of locomotives for presentation to railroad customers; using engineering drawings, he made preliminary sketches and final renderings. Patten also made styling contributions to GE diesel-electric industrial switchers (a 1937 80-ton model for Ford Motor Company, with a streamlined cab and chrome auto grilles; a 1939 60-ton for Mexico; and the 1940 65-ton standard model). His styling also appeared on the steam turbine–electric locomotive of 1939, and the so-called "Little Joe" electrics.

Arthur BecVar, who started in the Appearance Design Division in 1946, explained that Patten personally reviewed the work: "I was assigned to small appliances. Carl 'Fred' Schaus handled locomotives for Ray, then Bill Saenger took that assignment. I traveled to Erie with Saenger with models for 'workhorse' locomotives. The models for the streamlined locomotives went to Schenectady. If departments were outside Bridgeport, we would go there to meet with the engineering and marketing people."

BecVar became head of appearance design in 1948 after Patten's death. When GE built a separate manufacturing facility for major appliances in Louisville in 1951, BecVar and Saenger moved there. BecVar spent 33 years with GE before retiring.

Schaus, who was in the industrial products division in Schenectady, was primarily responsible for designing turbines, large motors and generators, switchgear, meters, and transformers. As a part-time consultant from 1950 to 1956, he conceived the contours and appearance of locomotives, as well as paint schemes. He traveled to Erie to get to know engineering managers and to see designs developed and built in the shop.

Schaus' designs included: GE diesel-electric locomotives of 1950 (1,500 horsepower for export with Alco engines and trucks); 1954 (a UD18 demonstrator for Mexico; the U9, U12, and U18 for export; and Erie demonstrator set No. 750); 1955 (XP24, 751 and 752, and U25B prototypes); and 1956 (U25B demonstrator with high nose); plus GE gas turbine–electrics for Union Pacific in 1948; the 4,500-horsepower experimental demonstrator 101 (UP 50); production turbines of 1952 and 1954; and the 8,500-horsepower turbines of 1958.

When Erie asked for more work than he had time for, Schaus suggested that it hire its own full-time industrial designer. James R. Chapin, the only industrial designer on the staff of locomotive engineering and marketing from 1956 to 1992, did all the appearance and ergonomic design for locomotives and multiple-unit commuter transit cars. John Gould prepared presentation paintings for railroad customers, and consultants did the renderings for transit car proposals.

Chapin's GE diesel road locomotives included: the 1961 U25B demonstrator paint scheme; the 1962 U25B and U25C low-nose cab design; the 1963 U50 cab for Union Pacific; the 1965 U50 C-C cab for Union Pacific; the 1967 U30CG passenger unit cab for Santa Fe; the 1978 BQ23-7 for Family Lines' first full-crew operator's cab; the 1980 C36-7 operator's cab; the 1982 C36-7 for China paint scheme; the 1983 C36-8 testbed; the 1986 DASH 8-40CM for Canadian National cab design and desktop operator consoles; the 1987 DASH 8-40CW North American Safety Cab; and the 1990 DASH 8-32BWH "Pepsi Can" for Amtrak.

Chapin's GE electric locomotives included: 1962's 4,200-horsepower units for Paulista Railway; the 1972 E60CP for Amtrak; the 1973 E-42C cab and paint scheme for Taiwan; the 1974 E60C cab and paint scheme for Mexico; and the 1975 E60C-2 cab and paint scheme for Deseret-Western. His GE industrial diesel-electric switchers were the 1974 standard switchers.

When Chapin retired in 1992, GE did not hire a replacement and has made made no substantial changes in the appearance of its road freight locomotives.

set up to oversee the allocation of strategic industrial materials for the war effort, took control of American locomotive production, limiting locomotive construction and reallocating some locomotive facilities and materials for military purposes. The War Production Board included representatives from various locomotive builders and significant parts suppliers to assist in the board's recommendations. The WPB divvied up locomotive production by type, in an effort to standardize procurement and, more importantly, to minimize problems with the production and supply of replacement parts.

The WPB directed the big steam builders—Alco, Baldwin, and Lima—to construct steam locomotives using established, tested designs, and the board greatly restricted the number of new designs. However, it also encouraged railroads to purchase steam locomotives, and severely curtailed diesel production in order to conserve crucial materials needed for military purposes. One valued commodity was copper, which is a primary component in electrical systems and traction motors. Since EMD had developed the most practical road freight locomotive, it was limited to the production of FTs. Baldwin and Alco were directed to build diesel-powered yard switchers and were largely restricted from selling road diesel models, although Alco was also allowed to produce some RS-1s and a few DL109s. Despite production limitations, there were no explicit restrictions on research and development, with the caveat that builders were not permitted to implement significant design changes on production models until the war's end.

After WPB restrictions were lifted, diesel builders scrambled to introduce new road models for North American railroads, as orders for steam locomotives dropped off sharply. EMD's line was at the forefront of the industry, followed by Alco-GE's. Both Baldwin and Fairbanks-Morse captured smaller amounts of the business. Alco-GE introduced several new models that used Alco's 244 engine, a design developed during the war. Like earlier Alco engines, the 244 was a four-cycle design. (The four cycles are: *intake*, the first downward piston stroke, in which air is forced into the cylinder; *compression*, the first upward stroke, in which air is compressed, greatly increasing the temperature; *power*, as the compression stroke nears completion, fuel is injected into the cylinder, igniting and forcing the piston downward; and *exhaust*, the second upward stroke in which burned gases are

expelled from the cylinder.) The 244 engine used GE's RD1 turbocharger originally developed during the war for aircraft applications. In its original configuration, the 12-cylinder 244 engine idled at 350 rpm and worked at full speed at 1,000 rpm to produce 1,500 horsepower. It was used to power Alco-GE carbody road freight locomotives (types later assigned FA-1/FB-1 model designations; the latter a cabless booster) and RS-2 road switchers, models introduced to compete with EMD's F-units. John Kirkland indicates that the early FA models (specification numbers DL208 and DL209) used GE's GT564B traction generator and were equipped with either GE 726 or GE 731 traction motors. Using a standard 74:18 gear ratio, they were designed for 65 miles per hour maximum speed and would deliver 34,000 pounds continuous tractive effort at 13.5 miles per hour. These locomotives employed belt-driven auxiliary equipment. More advanced FA/FBs, (beginning with specification numbers DL208A and DL209B) and RS-2s (beginning with specification E1661A) were built starting in 1947. These later locomotives dispensed with belt-driven auxiliaries and employed more reliable motor-driven equipment. The traction generator type was upgraded to GE's GT564C model, and the GE 752 traction motor was introduced. This successful traction motor design has been a fundamental component used by thousands of GE locomotives since. Using the improved traction system greatly boosted tractive effort: FA/FBs with GE 752 motors delivered 42,550 pounds of continuous tractive effort at 11 miles per hour. In early 1950, Alco boosted the output of its 12-cylinder 244 engine to 1,600 horsepower, corresponding to like increases in power from Baldwin and Fairbanks-Morse. Later FA/FBs and RS-2s thus featured the higher rating. In mid-1950, Alco changed the model designation of its 1,600-horsepower road-switcher type from RS-2 to RS-3. Despite the change, the locomotives were virtually the same. Alco-GE's RS-3 operator's manual from September 1951 lists locomotive specifications:

Maximum height: 14 feet, 5-1/8 inches
Maximum width: 10 feet, 1-5/8 inches
Length (inside knuckles): 55 feet, 11-3/4 inches
Weight on drivers: 240,000 pounds

Alco's RS-2 and RS-3 road switchers were versatile machines designed to work singly or in multiple in freight, passenger, and switching service. They featured a semi-streamlined hood-unit configuration that was one of the more attractive road-switcher designs. Several railroads favored RS-2/RS-3s for suburban passenger operations, because they accelerated quickly and could maintain schedules better than other types. The Boston & Maine, New York Central, New Haven, Long Island, Pennsylvania, Reading, Erie, Central Railroad of New Jersey, and Rock Island all employed suburban service RS-2/RS-3 fleets.

In summer 1946, Alco-GE introduced a new high-horsepower, handsomely streamlined passenger locomotive that we today know as the Alco PA. Initially, Alco-GE did not use the PA/PB designations, instead describing these locomotives by their specification numbers. (The designation PA stands for Passenger, A-unit; the PB designation was used to describe the cabless booster.) The PA/PB was a full-carbody locomotive type that shared basic design elements with the Alco's FA freight diesel and embodied a well-balanced look. It featured a 6-foot-long "nose" section and used three-axle, four-motor trucks in an A1A configuration. (The center axle was unpowered for weight distribution.) John Kirkland indicates the PA measured 65 feet, 8 inches long over the couplers, while period sources give a slightly longer measurement of 66 feet, 2 inches.

Many observers have deemed Alco's PA as one of the finest-looking passenger locomotives of all time. Initially, the type was powered by a 16-cylinder 244 diesel using GE's RD2 turbocharger, which produced 2,000 horsepower. (Alco's primary competition was EMD's E-unit, which used a pair of 567 diesels instead of a single engine.) According to John Kirkland, the early PAs employed GE 746A2 traction motors and the GT566C1 traction generator. During the course of PA production, which ran from 1946 to 1953, Alco-GE introduced several improvements, including the GE 752 traction motor and a 250-horsepower increase per unit, giving the later PAs (often designated PA-2) a 2,250-horsepower rating. A total of 297 PAs were built for 16 different American railways. Among the type's best-known buyers were the Santa Fe, Southern Pacific, New York Central, Pennsylvania Railroad, New Haven, Lehigh Valley, and Erie.

During the massive postwar dieselization of American railroads, Alco-GE consistently held the position of number two diesel builder, with EMD remaining as the clear

industry leader. However, according to Albert Churella in his book, *From Steam to Diesel*, Alco-GE commanded roughly 40 percent of the diesel-electric market in 1946, but slipped to only 15 percent by 1953. Churella illustrates a number of causes for this dramatic loss of business, some of which were a result of Alco's steam-era business practices. There were also issues of locomotive reliability. Although Alco-GE locomotives enjoyed favorable performance characteristics, offering higher horsepower per unit and greater tractive effort than comparable EMD products, many railroads found that Alco diesels required more maintenance than EMD products. A number of flaws were attributed to the 244 engine design, which was phased out in the mid-1950s when Alco introduced its more reliable 251 diesel engine. There were also difficulties with GE's Amplidyne electrical system. While Amplidyne control was intended to give a locomotive engineer more precise tractive control, it was more complex to operate than other "hands-off" electrical systems.

In 1953, GE terminated its joint production agreement with Alco, although the company continued to supply Alco with electrical gear for its diesel-electric locomotives. General Electric also continued to provide electrical gear for other builders, such as Fairbanks-Morse. Interestingly, while the Alco-GE arrangement was at its peak in the immediate postwar period, GE also built Fairbanks-Morse road diesels under contract at its Erie, Pennsylvania, plant. These large carbody locomotives were often known as Fairbanks-Morse *Erie-Builts*, to distinguish them from later locomotives built by Fairbanks-Morse at its Beloit, Wisconsin, factory. The Erie-Builts shared several common characteristics with the Alco-GE PA, which was designed about the same time.

GE Switchers

General Electric's original diesel locomotive market was for lightweight, low-output switcher types, and despite its agreement with Alco in the production of road locomotives, GE continued to produce its own line of switchers. In 1940, GE introduced new standard switcher models. The two most popular types used by domestic railroads were the 44-ton center-cab model and the 70-ton end-cab model. The 44-ton model was designed to comply with late 1930s legislation that permitted single-man operation

of locomotives weighing less than 90,000 pounds (45 U.S. tons). Heavier locomotives required both an engineer and fireman. Although several manufacturers built small center-cab switchers, GE's were the most common. Since the 44-ton label was a model designation, actual weight and output varied somewhat depending on individual locomotive configuration. The typical 44-tonner was powered by a pair of Caterpillar D17000 diesel engines, one at each end of the locomotive. These engines were rated between 180 and 200 horsepower each, providing between 360 and 400 total horsepower. The compact four-cycle V-8 design had a 5-3/4x8-inch bore and stroke and worked at maximum 1,000 rpm. A few 44-tonners used other engine types. A number of American Class I railroads, including the Boston & Maine, Pennsylvania Railroad, Santa Fe, and Burlington, employed 44-tonners in switching service, especially on light branchlines and industrial trackage, where heavier locomotives would damage track and

bridges. Shortline railroads embraced the type, using them to replace steam locomotives.

Numerous electric interurban railways had operated freight service over portions of their passenger lines, although by the 1940s many had dropped unprofitable passenger service and retained their freight operations. The 44-ton diesel-electric was an economical motive power solution for these lines. Many industrial lines and private companies also had GE center-cab switchers, including the 44-ton model. More than 350 44-tonners were built between 1940 and 1956.

The 70-tonner was designed for branchline work and allowed for relatively fast operation on very light track. Like the 44-tonner, it was acquired by both Class I and shortline railroads, where it was used to replace lightweight steam locomotives. Often 70-tonners were used where heavier diesels were banned because of weight restrictions. The 70-tonner was powered by a single six-cylinder Cooper-Bessemer

Allegheny Ludlum Steel Company's 65-ton GE switcher No. 18 makes a transfer run between its Natrona and Brackenridge, Pennsylvania, plants on May 13, 1988. Allegheny Ludlum hosts a fleet of radio-controlled GE center-cab locomotives. By the early 1980s, General Electric had built more than 5,700 diesel-electric switchers for use by railways and industrial customers in North America and around the world. *Patrick Yough*

57

FWL6T diesel—the engine later developed by GE into the 7FDL-16—the prime mover used in most of its modern diesels. General Electric introduced its 70-tonner in 1946, and built more than 130 of them for the North American market over the next dozen years.

GE also built a great variety of switchers for industrial and military applications, as well as export. These ranged from small 25-ton units to locomotives weighing 110 tons or more. They were built to suit lines with a variety of different track gauges, and included a narrow gauge model for both industrial and shortline use. Although often eclipsed by GE's large, powerful, and high-profile locomotives, switchers were an important part of GE's locomotive business for many years. By the 1970s it had built more than 5,000 of them for service in

dozens of countries around the world. In 1944 and 1945, GE built 30 45-ton center-cab switchers for service in India. Similar to domestic types, these locomotives were 33 feet, 11 inches long and were powered by a pair of 190-horsepower Caterpillar diesels. They used four GE733 traction motors and a GT555 traction generator, and delivered 23,500 pounds starting tractive effort.

As most railways completed dieselization in the 1950s, the need for new switching locomotives dropped off. Switchers tend to have very long life spans, as evidenced by some of the earliest diesels that could still be found working more than 40 years after they were built. Also, the need for specialized lightweight engines declined as large railroads either abandoned branchlines or improved weight limits to

allow for the operation of heavier locomotives. The gradual shift from traditional carload traffic to intermodal operations, and the disappearance of traditional heavy industries such as steelworks, has also reduced the need for switchers.

In 1974, GE introduced a new line of industrial center-cab switchers. It offered three basic models for the domestic market: the SL80, SL110, and SL144—designations that roughly indicate the maximum weight in U.S. tons of each type. These locomotives have a more angular and utilitarian appearance than similar models from the 1940s and 1950s. Based on production figures published in *The Contemporary Diesel Spotter's Guide*, the combined domestic production for the three models over a 12-year period was just over 50 locomotives. In addition to its basic offering, GE built a variety of modern specialized switchers that varied in weight and

output to meet individual customer requirements. A pair of Cummins diesel engines powered nearly all of GE's late-era switching locomotives.

According to GE's specifications, the SL144 measures 45 feet long; 13 feet, 3 inches tall; and 9 feet, 6 inches wide, making it shorter, lower, and narrower than any modern American road locomotive. The locomotive can weigh between 230,000 and 288,000 pounds (115 to 144 U.S. tons) depending on the customer's needs. At the minimum weight, the locomotive will produce 69,000 pounds starting tractive effort. Most of the 1974 line switchers were purchased by industrial railways and have only made rare appearances on larger lines. GE has built very few switchers in recent years, and instead has focused locomotive production on its successful road locomotive line.

In modern times, General Electric has offered several center-cab models for industrial switching. The SL80, SL110, and SL140 models began production in the mid-1970s. This switcher is operated by GE's own East Erie Commercial Railroad. *Author collection, photographer unknown*

TURBINES

Steam Turbine–Electric

The sudden and spectacular emergence of diesel-powered, high-speed streamlined passenger trains in the mid-1930s captured the collective imagination of American railroads. The novelty of new power sources and streamlining were the modes of the period, and they resulted in reactionary technological development as well as refinement in diesel-electric technology. General Motors' Electro-Motive Corporation was the driving force behind the development of internal combustion streamliners. In the spirit of these fast new trains, starting in 1936, General Electric worked with Union Pacific in the design and development of a "steam-electric locomotive," an oil-fired steam turbine–electric. General Electric planned to meld established stationary and marine steam turbine technology with electric locomotive designs to produce a new type of locomotive. Early GE specifications called for a streamlined turbine-electric locomotive with a net input of 2,500 horsepower "to the electric transmission for traction," and the ability to produce 81,000 pounds starting tractive effort. In GE lexicon, each unit was designated a 2-C-C-2–318/506–6GE725. The first part of the designation indicated the wheel arrangement (two guiding axles, two sets of three powered axles, and two trailing axles), while the last part reflected the traction motor arrangement of six GE 725 motors.

Opposite: General Electric's first gas turbine locomotive was a 4,500-horsepower double-cab unit numbered Union Pacific 50. It is portrayed here with a train of Pacific Fruit Express refrigerator cars at Sloan, Nevada, on Union Pacific's Los Angeles–Salt Lake route. Later gas turbines built for UP only had cabs at one end. *Union Pacific photo, John Gruber collection*

Initially, GE hoped to deliver the prototype steam-electric locomotive in 1937, but the machines were not ready for testing by Union Pacific until spring 1939. At that time the steam-electric locomotive attracted considerable attention in the trade press. Some viewed it as a potential successor to conventional reciprocating steam locomotive technology, as well as a challenge to the new diesel-electrics and an alternative to electrification. In the February 1939 issue of *General Electric Review*, the turbine was touted as having twice the thermal efficiency of a conventional steam locomotive and capable of operating at 125 miles per hour.

Two streamlined 2,500-horsepower units were built and designed to operate "elephant style," as opposed to back to back. Each machine weighed 548,000 pounds fully loaded, with 354,000 pounds on driving wheels, resulting in a 59,000-pound maximum axle load and allowing each unit to produce 86,500 pounds starting tractive effort, slightly more than originally specified. Continuous tractive effort had two ratings, depending on the amount of air supplied to cool traction motors: 32,000 pounds tractive effort with normal cooling or 40,500 pounds with greater cooling.

The locomotive used a 65:31 gear ratio to power 44-inch-diameter driving wheels. Guide and trailing wheels were just 36 inches in diameter.

The two locomotives featured styled and streamlined carbodies that shared a resemblance to EMC's Union Pacific streamliners of the period. The body was a lightweight truss type that used welded low-carbon, high-tensile steel frame supports and was covered with riveted sheet metal. Most of the skin and secondary supports were made from aluminum, except those used on the nose section, which were made of steel. An elevated cab was employed, similar to that used in EMC's M-10003 to M-10006 articulated *City* streamliners, and subsequently by E-unit passenger locomotives. This height afforded the operating crew a good forward view, while the substantial 9-foot nose section, which was significantly longer than that used by General Motors products, afforded protection in the event of a collision. Both sides of the nose also featured prominently placed General Electric builder's plates. Each unit measured 90 feet, 10 inches long and 15 feet, 3/4 inch tall, and was 10 feet wide at the cab.

A pair of General Electric steam turbine–electrics, Union Pacific Nos. 1 and 2, make their first run westward on UP's Lane Cutoff, west of Omaha, Nebraska, in April 1939. *Union Pacific photo, John Gruber collection*

The design of the steam turbine was largely based on contemporary powerplant technology of the time. Each unit employed a Babcock & Wilcox water-tube boiler that was fired and regulated automatically by specialized equipment built by the Bailey Meter Company. The boiler operated at 1,500 psi and 920 degrees Fahrenheit. By comparison, a late-era "superpower" steam locomotive, such as Union Pacific's own 800 series 4-8-4s, used a fire-tube boiler and had an operating pressure of just 300 psi. By removing impurities from the water and keeping it in a closed circuit, scale buildup was greatly reduced and the amount of water needed to operate the locomotive was kept at a minimum. Despite the closed circuit, there was some water loss during the heating cycle, and replenishment water was stored in tanks located in the locomotive nose section. Enough fuel oil was stored in tanks at the back of the locomotive to operate 500 to 700 miles between refueling.

Normally, the turbines worked at 12,500 rpm and turned a generator set using 10:1 reduction gearing. The generator set consisted of a self-ventilated, twin-armature DC generator to provide electricity for the traction motors;

a 220-volt, three-phase AC generator provided power for auxiliaries such as traction motor blowers and head-end power. (See discussion below.) The locomotives were equipped with dynamic braking, which used traction motors as generators. Today, dynamic brakes are standard on most diesel electric locomotives, but at the time of the steam turbine, the concept was unusual. Unlike modern diesel-locomotives, which expend all of the energy generated by dynamic braking, steam turbine locomotives directed water through resistor grids that allowed the locomotive to recoup some of the energy generated during periods of heavy braking.

The head-end power generator was also decades ahead of its time. Head-end electrical power is used to provide electricity to passenger cars for heat, light, and air conditioning. Most American passenger equipment continued to use conventional steam heat through the 1970s, and as a result many passenger diesels were equipped with steam generators. Only with the coming of Amtrak was steam heat finally dispensed with in favor of head-end power, which is now standard.

Union Pacific paraded the new GE steam turbines around the United States with a vintage 4-4-0 American-type steam locomotive to promote Paramount's 1939 film *Union Pacific*, which told the story of the building of the first transcontinental railroad. The film premiered at Omaha on the eve of the 70th anniversary of the Golden Spike Ceremony that joined the Union Pacific and the Central Pacific at Promontory, Utah, on May 10, 1869. *Union Pacific photo, John Gruber collection*

Officials pose with General Electric's steam turbine–electric at Erie, Pennsylvania, on October 24, 1938. When this machine was built, GE had great hopes for it; the steam turbine–electric was heralded as the successor to the traditional steam locomotive and a competitor of the diesel. *Union Pacific photo, John Gruber collection*

The steam-electric locomotives were delivered to Union Pacific in time for celebrations commemorating the seventieth anniversary of the completion of the first transcontinental railroad, which had occurred in May 1869. Union Pacific employed the locomotives on special trains that toured the railroad, giving the public a glimpse of them while providing railroad officials with a chance to see how they performed in service. In addition to service on the UP, the locomotives also made a tour of East Coast cities, traveling over the New York Central, New Haven, and Pennsylvania lines with a special UP train. The turbines featured excellent acceleration and maintained schedules faster than conventional steam-powered trains, but exhibited a variety of small failures. Most of these shortcomings were quickly corrected, but they discouraged Union Pacific officials, who became impatient with the turbines' failings.

Union Pacific considered using the turbines on a premier transcontinental passenger run but questioned their reliability. After just a couple of months of road testing in both passenger and perishable freight service, Union Pacific returned the locomotives to GE in June 1939, in the words of UP president W. M. Jeffers, "for necessary modification and/or reconstruction." Union Pacific remained interested in the steam-electrics for another two years, and Jeffers wrote that he believed the basic design principles were valid and the locomotives could be made to operate sufficiently reliably for UP's intended service. However, in December 1941, UP terminated its arrangement with GE. Among the reasons

cited for the change of position on the steam-electrics were what Jeffers described as "developments in other types of motive power." Specifically, Jeffers was referring to Union Pacific's 4-8-8-4 "Big Boy" type of steam locomotive, Electro-Motive's improved E-units, and the recently debuted FT freight diesels. Another factor in Union Pacific's waning interest in the steam-electrics may have been a regime change in the railroad's motive power department in the spring of 1939.

Despite Union Pacific's dissatisfaction with the steam-electrics, GE continued to work on them. In 1941, the locomotives operated in test service on the New York Central, primarily on its Water Level Route in New York State. Then in 1943, during the World War II power crunch, Great Northern operated the steam-electrics in heavy freight service between Spokane and Wenatchee, Washington. An article by Thomas R. Lee in Volume 10, Number 2, of *The Streamliner* indicates that by this time the turbines had been renumbered GE-1 and GE-2 and painted in a grayish black livery. Several sources, including *The Streamliner*, indicate the turbines provided good service on the GN. Steam locomotive historian Alfred W. Bruce concludes in his book *The Steam Locomotive in America* that GE's steam-electric was "one of the most exceptional steam locomotives ever built, and should be recognized as a pioneer because of its conception, design, and construction." Although GE shelved its steam turbine–electric some 60 years ago, the basic premise for this type of locomotive may someday be revived. Steam turbine technology has matured since the 1940s, and modern microprocessor technologies allow for a high level of precision control.

Gas Turbines

In the postwar environment, General Electric began development of a gas turbine locomotive type which, like the steam turbine, also attracted Union Pacific's interest. In 1948, GE built experimental double-ended gas turbine–electric No. 101, which became the prototype for one of the world's most unusual locomotive fleets. General Electric was neither the first to experiment with gas turbines nor the first to build a gas turbine locomotive, but it was the only company to build a fleet of them for heavy North American freight service. For decades, gas turbines had been built for use as stationary power plants. In *Modern Railway Locomotives*, P. Ransome-Wallis explains that since the 1920s various European locomotive builders had experimented with gas turbine locomotives. A successful machine was demonstrated in 1943, when Swiss manufacturer Brown Boveri unveiled a gas turbine with a 1-D-1 arrangement for Swiss Federal Railways.

Above: Union Pacific's 4,500-horsepower gas turbine locomotive No. 54 is seen in the shop, when the locomotive was brand-new. The equipment in front of the locomotive is a turbine power unit, presumably for No. 54. *Union Pacific photo, John Gruber collection*

Left: Union Pacific's first 10 production turbines were very similar to the prototype (GE 101, later Union Pacific No. 50), except they featured cabs only at one end. These machines were delivered in 1952 and numbered from 51 to 60. Turbine No. 60 is seen with a fuel tender and two Union Pacific EMD-built GP9s leading a westbound freight at sunset. *Otto Perry, Denver Public Library Western History Department*

By the late 1940s, the clear superiority of diesel-electric locomotives had sealed the fate of steam on most American railways, and Union Pacific was still looking for greater single-unit power than contemporary diesels could deliver. By virtue of its double-track route and relatively easy crossing of the Continental Divide, UP's mainline was, and is, one of America's primary east-west freight corridors. Across the Nebraska cornfields and the plains of Wyoming, Union Pacific freights can roll along largely unhindered for hundreds of miles. Even UP's grades in Wyoming and Utah are relatively mild in comparison to other transcontinental routes. It was in this wide-open territory that the gas turbine locomotive offered an advantage over diesel-electric operation. For two years Union Pacific tested the prototype, which was repainted for Union Pacific and designated UP No. 50. The railroad operated it for an estimated 106,000 miles in heavy service while General Electric worked out technical bugs and design hiccups. The locomotive's boxy-streamlined carbody design resembled those of Alco-GE cab diesels and GE's straight electric locomotives. It was 83 feet, 7-1/2 inches long; slightly more than 15 feet, 4 inches tall; 10 feet, 7 inches wide; and weighed an estimated 500,000 pounds. The locomotive used a B-B+B-B wheel arrangement, and its basic 4,500-horsepower rating (see below) was more than twice that available from single-unit diesel-electrics of the period. It delivered 77,800 pounds continuous tractive effort at 18.2 miles per hour.

The locomotive was powered by a GE gas turbine derived from contemporary aircraft engine design. It also employed a 15-stage axial flow compressor that directed airflow in a linear fashion along the shaft to compress filtered intake air to six atmospheres and then into six combustion chambers. The chambers were arranged radially around a central axis that contained the turbine shaft. Within the combustion chambers, compressed air was blended with fuel to burn at 1,400 degrees Fahrenheit (760 degrees Celsius), and the resulting gas was then directed through a two-stage (two sets of blades) turbine. Exhaust gases exited the turbine through roof vents at 850 degrees Fahrenheit at a speed of 150 miles per hour when operating under full load.

The output shaft was directly connected to the axial flow compressor and turbine, which turned four GE-576 electrical generators through a system of speed reduction gearing with a 65:18 gear ratio, allowing for 69 miles per

Top: A pair of 1952-built gas turbines brackets a fuel tender on a long westbound freight. These two turbines had a combined output of 9,000 horsepower; Union Pacific put them to work moving heavy freight over long distances at high speeds. Contemporary reports indicated the turbines could accelerate faster than diesel-electrics. Turbines burned low-grade petroleum, known as Bunker C oil, which was much cheaper than diesel fuel when the turbines were purchased. *Otto Perry, Denver Public Library Western History Department*

Above: Union Pacific's second order of GE turbines was numbered from 61 to 75. Mechanically, these were similar to the first order, but featured external catwalks that earned them the nickname "veranda turbines." The first of these, No. 61, is seen leading a freight with a fuel tender and a pair of EMD GP9s. *Otto Perry, Denver Public Library Western History Department*

Beginning in 1958, General Electric built for Union Pacific a fleet of more-advanced gas turbines that were rated at 8,500 horsepower. These later turbines were built in two pieces. Brand-new turbine No. 1/1B is seen with a fuel tender and a long freight under clear western skies. *Union Pacific photo, John Gruber collection*

hour maximum speed. (Reduction gearing was required because turbine output was greater than economically practical for electrical generation.) The gas turbine locomotive's electrical transmission system was very similar to that used by contemporary diesel-electrics and, in fact, used many common components, including traction motors. The GE-576 generators powered eight standard GE 752 nose-suspended traction motors, one for each axle.

Ambient temperature and atmospheric pressure affects turbine performance. As elevation increases, atmospheric pressure drops and turbine output decreases. Although Union Pacific No. 50's nominal output was rated at 4,500 horsepower, this must be clarified for accuracy. Technically, it generated 4,800 horsepower, when at its full load of 6,700 rpm, when working at 1,500 feet above sea level, with an ambient temperature of 80 degrees Fahrenheit. Of this output, 300 horsepower powered auxiliary functions, thus leaving 4,500 horsepower for traction. The locomotive used a six-cylinder Cooper-Bessemer diesel to provide auxiliary power for starting the turbine and moving the locomotive at slow speeds when gas turbine propulsion was not cost-effective.

A gas turbine locomotive only performs at optimum efficiency when operating at maximum load; compared with diesels, efficiency falls off dramatically when turbine speed is decreased. Union Pacific hoped to obtain cost-effective operation with the gas turbine locomotives by using them exclusively on long-haul heavy freight runs, where the machines could make the most of their enormous output. At maximum output, the gas turbine's fuel consumption was roughly twice that of a diesel locomotive set of similar output. Offsetting the turbine's high fuel consumption was the fact that it burned very cheap Bunker C fuel oil, the heavy oil that remains after high-value oils like gasoline and diesel have been distilled from crude petroleum. In order for the gas turbine to burn Bunker C, the oil needed to be heated to 200 degrees Fahrenheit and filtered prior to combustion, and the turbine was only fired on Bunker C oil after it had been brought up to speed using diesel fuel.

By 1950, GE and UP were sufficiently satisfied with the performance of the experimental turbine to put a fleet of locomotives in regular service. Among the advantages of gas turbine operation were greater output for the weight and length of the locomotive as compared with diesel-electrics, simpler mechanical components than diesel-electric locomotives (leading UP to anticipate greater reliability and lower maintenance costs), lower overall fuel costs, and the rapid acceleration of heavy trains.

Initially UP ordered 10 gas turbines, but placed a second order for 15 additional machines before the first batch was delivered in January 1952. The production locomotives were similar to the prototype, except they featured just a single-cab design. The first 10, numbered 51 to 60, featured a full carbody design. The subsequent 15 machines, delivered in 1954, incorporated technological advances and featured

Union Pacific's 8,500-horsepower turbine No. 2/2B is seen near Echo, Utah, in 1958. The later turbines used a pair of C-C units with a total of 12 traction motors. They were primarily assigned to Overland Route trains, on which UP could make the most of their high output. *Union Pacific photo, John Gruber collection*

external catwalks along the sides of the locomotive. For this reason, these machines, numbered 61 to 75, were popularly known as *veranda turbines*. They were 83 feet, 6 inches long, weighed 551,000 pounds, rode on 40-inch wheels, and produced 105,000 pounds continuous tractive effort (speed not indicated).

By 1957, UP boasted that as much as 11-1/2 percent of all its freight traffic was hauled by the gas turbine fleet. Turbines were primarily assigned to UP's main trunk, the heavily traveled Overland Route between Omaha, Nebraska, and Ogden, Utah. The most difficult challenges were the 0.82 percent westward ruling grade over Sherman Hill west of Cheyenne, Wyoming, and the eastward ascent of Utah's Weber and Echo Canyons. According to an article by Lester C. Harlow in the February 1955 issue of *Railroad Magazine*, turbine No. 57 hauled a 91-car freight weighing 4,200 tons between Rawlins and Green River, Utah, over the Continental Divide. He noted the working turbines produced enormous noise and described them as sounding something like a steam locomotive having its boiler blown down. The turbine's deafening roar earned them the name "Big Blows" by most railroaders. Their unacceptably high noise levels also proved a limiting factor in their operation.

Despite some difficulties, UP was sufficiently pleased with GE's gas turbines to invest in another 30 units of a more advanced design in the mid-1950s. These locomotives were bought in part to replace its 25 Big Boy steam locomotives that were reaching retirement age. Built in 1958, the later turbines used a two-section carbody arrangement with each section riding on C-C floating bolster trucks. The two sections measured a total of 132 feet, 6 inches long. In addition to the driver's cab and locomotive control equipment, the first section contained the auxiliary diesel engine and electrical generator, diesel fuel tank, batteries, air compressor and air reservoir (for braking), and dynamic braking resistor grids. The second unit contained the gas turbine, main traction generators, and related equipment. These machines employed a substantially more powerful gas turbine that featured a 16-stage axial flow compressor, 10 combustion chambers, and a two-stage turbine.

The arrangement of equipment was somewhat different. With the older turbines, the power shaft came out of the exhaust casing, but on the new machines the power shaft exited on the compressor end of the turbine. Full load was achieved at 4,860 rpm. These gas turbines were almost twice as powerful as the first-generation machines and their service condition rating was 8,500 horsepower at 6,000 feet above sea level with an ambient temperature of 90 degrees Fahrenheit. In an article in the May 1957 issue of *Diesel Railway Traction*, General Electric's R.M. Smith compares the output of the two turbine types, explaining that at 1,500 feet above sea level and 80 degrees Fahrenheit, the newer turbines could produce a nominal rating of 10,700 horsepower. He also notes, however, that the machines only had sufficient electrical capacity to accommodate 8,500 horsepower. To overcome complaints of inadequate control with the earlier turbines, the 8,500-horsepower machines used a 20-notch air-actuated driver's throttle. As with the 4,500-horsepower locomotives, the 8,500-horsepower gas turbines employed four generators operating at 1,050 rpm each, reduced from the turbine power shaft through gearing.

However, instead of eight traction motors on the 4,500-horsepower units, these generators powered 12 GE 752 traction motors, each engaging one axle using a 74:18 gear ratio. With this gearing combined with 40-inch wheels, the 8,500-horsepower gas turbines were designed for 65-mile-per-hour operation. Ransome-Wallis indicates they delivered 240,000 pounds starting tractive effort and 145,000 pounds continuous tractive effort at 18 miles per hour. By comparison, a single 1,500-horsepower Alco FA-1 weighing 228,500 pounds and using 40-inch wheels and a 74:18 gear ratio delivered 60,000 pounds starting tractive effort and 34,000 pounds continuous tractive effort at 13-1/2 miles per hour.

Another change on the later turbines was the pre-filtering of Bunker C oil rather than filtering fuel on board the locomotive. To give the turbines greater range between refueling, Union Pacific equipped them with 23,000-gallon fuel tenders remanufactured from steam locomotive tenders.

The Gas Turbine's Demise

Although Union Pacific built an experimental coal-fired gas turbine in 1959, ultimately it gave up on its gas turbine fleet in favor of modern diesel-electric locomotives. A variety of factors contributed to the turbine's demise. Turbine efficiency drops dramatically when operated at less than full load, so when UP was not keeping trains at top speeds, turbines were much less efficient than diesel-electrics, which were still reasonably efficient at slower speeds. Although the gas turbines were supposed to offer greater reliability and lower maintenance costs, an article by Union Pacific's Ross C. Hill in the July 1957 issue of *Diesel Railway Traction* suggests otherwise. In his article, Hill states that the 4,500-horsepower turbine's reliability was hampered by a variety of auxiliary system failures. More serious problems, the article says, included blade erosion in the main axial flow compressors that required re-blading after about every 15,000 hours of service. The use of Bunker C oil was also a difficulty. The ability to burn this cheap oil had been anticipated as one of the primary advantages of the GE turbines, but the fuel proved difficult to burn and caused greater wear to turbine blades than more refined fuel. Today, operators of stationary turbines would only consider Bunker C oil as a fuel of last resort.

Finally, by the 1960s, significant improvements in diesel-electric technology closed the performance gap between gas turbines and diesels. Diesel engines were improved to burn lower grades of fuel than had been possible in the 1940s. By 1960, GE had entered the heavy diesel-electric business, and 4,500-horsepower gas turbines were traded in for U50 diesels in 1963. The 8,500-horsepower turbines met a similar fate a few years later, when they were turned in for GE U50Cs.

Union Pacific's 8,500-horsepower turbines used the common GE 752 traction motor. More modern variants of this standard motor can be found beneath modern General Electric DC-traction diesels. *Union Pacific photo, John Gruber collection*

Union Pacific gas turbine No. 11/11B leads an EMD DD35 and two DD35Bs (eight-motor double-diesels) eastbound near Hermosa, Wyoming, as a westbound train passes on the lower track. *Union Pacific photo, John Gruber collection*

UNIVERSAL LINE

Geneial Electric was one of the foremost suppliers of electrical components for locomotives during the formative years of American dieselization, and a significant producer of lightweight diesel-electric switchers and industrial locomotives. As previously described, GE worked closely with Alco from 1940 until 1953 in the production and marketing of heavy diesel-electric locomotive designs. The three decades following the introduction of Central Railroad of New Jersey No. 1000 saw revolutionary change in the American locomotive market. The diesel had evolved from an experimental switching locomotive into *the* preferred and dominant machine for railroad transport. In the early 1940s, when Alco and GE had cemented their relationship, the situation was still in flux. While the diesel-electric had demonstrated great capability, some in the industry believed that there was still a place for steam locomotives alongside diesels, while for others the large-scale electrification of American railways seemed to be just on the horizon.

At the time, the diesel-electric was seen as the latest form of motive power, but still too new to declare the greatest. Despite this view, the overwhelming superiority of diesel power for American heavy-haul applications resulted in an unprecedented wide-scale switch from steam to diesel power. In the March 1947 issue of *Diesel Railway Traction,* it was noted that Alco had spent an estimated $20 million on the

Opposite: Erie-Lackawanna U33C No. 3308 sits at an engine terminal in Port Jervis, New York. General Electric built 16 U33Cs for Erie-Lackawanna in the late 1960s. *Jim Shaughnessy*

research and development of diesel-electric locomotives and expected that 93 percent of its production capacity would be in diesel-electric manufacturing. But even as railroads undertook large-scale dieselization at a rate faster than even optimistic estimates had anticipated, many projected that steam power would still be in use through the mid-1960s.

Albert Churella, author of the book *From Steam to Diesel*, notes that as late as 1947, even Alco executives still believed that a portion of their business would be derived from the production of steam power. By 1954, however, dieselization was nearing completion; several large railroads were already completely dieselized and most were only a few years away from dispensing with their last steam locomotives. Even Norfolk & Western, America's last large steam holdout, was on the verge of abandoning steam. Serious talk of large-scale electrification had quieted.

During this steam-to-diesel transition, Electro-Motive had become America's largest locomotive supplier, producing the vast majority of diesel locomotives while traditional locomotive builders fell on hard times. As dieselization neared completion in the mid-1950s, there was a sharp decline in the new locomotive market, forcing out the weakest builders, Baldwin and Fairbanks-Morse. Railroads had embraced the many operational advantages of diesel-electric

operation, including much lower maintenance costs; substantially better thermal efficiency, which translated to lower fuel costs; and the fact that they were less damaging to track. In addition, the ability to operate diesels in multiple, combined with high tractive effort from a start, allowed the railroads to operate much longer and heavier trains.

Locomotive manufacturers had offered a variety of diesel models to suit railroads' various needs. Switching engines were built for light work; streamlined cab units were built for freight and passenger work; high-speed passenger diesels, such as the EMD E-unit and Alco PA, were designed for streamlined passenger services; and heavy, slow-speed transfer locomotives had been built for heavy yard transfers and mineral service. By the late 1940s, the road-switcher type was gaining popularity, and by the 1950s EMD's "General Purpose" road-switcher types had become the best-selling locomotives in the United States. In the late 1950s, railroads were clamoring for higher-horsepower general-purpose types that would provide operational flexibility while requiring fewer locomotives to haul heavy trains.

Fast freight service was the premier market as railroads faced ever-greater highway competition. EMD and Alco introduced new high-power designs in the late 1950s in response to market demands. These models were largely

General Electric's experimental diesel-electrics built in 1954 were painted for the Erie Railroad, where they operated for several years. The four-unit A-B-B-A set leads an eastbound freight toward Hornell at Canaseraga, New York, on Erie's Hornell-to-Buffalo mainline. These locomotives used Cooper-Bessemer diesel engines and were a precursor to the Universal Line. Later, they were re-powered and sold to Union Pacific as UM20Bs. *General Electric photo, William D. Middleton collection*

adaptations of existing designs, as the essential technology had not evolved much since the late 1930s. By that time, many of the oldest diesels—those sold during World War II and in the immediate postwar period—were reaching the end of their expected service lives. To sell new models, Alco and EMD encouraged railroads to trade in older locomotives as credit on new ones.

General Electric Diesel Development

In reaction to industry developments, General Electric made a well-timed entry in to the American heavy locomotive market. In 1953, GE formally dissolved its arrangement with Alco on the production of road locomotives and began developing its own locomotive line. Perhaps no other North American company was in a better position to develop a locomotive than GE. The company had all the resources it needed on hand: large-scale locomotive construction facilities, excellent locomotive engineering experience, and sufficient financial resources to fund research and development. Unlike Alco and EMD, which were battling for immediate market share, GE could take the time to develop locomotive technology free from immediate competitive forces. Competitive pressures had rushed diesel development in the 1940s, resulting in design errors.

GE's engineers surveyed experienced railroaders to learn their views about the performance and reliability of contemporary diesel locomotives. Using this input, they looked to provide a better locomotive, and undoubtedly hoped to avoid some of the problems that plagued Alco, Fairbanks-Morse, and Baldwin products. General Electric

In the mid-1950s, General Electric debuted its Universal Line, which directly competed with both Alco and EMD for lucrative export sales. General Electric's primary export markets were in Third World countries that did not possess railway technology of their own. A GE U11B is seen at the Pacific Railway Station in San Jose, Costa Rica, on the Ferrocarriles de Costa Rica. *William D. Middleton*

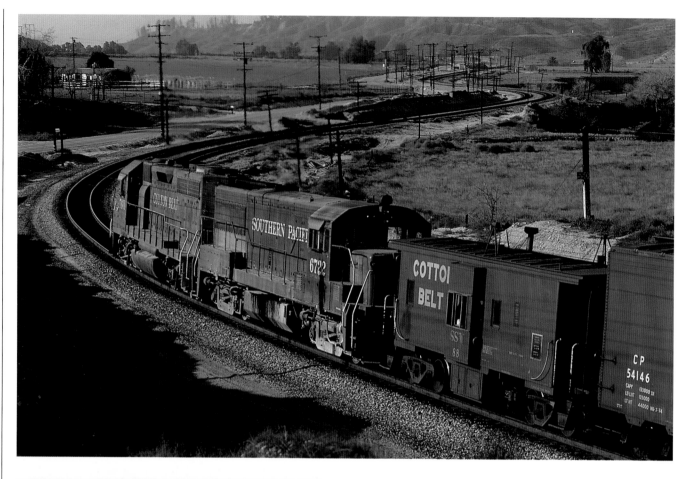

designers sought to build a better, simpler, and potentially more powerful locomotive than any available on the American market at that time.

David P. Morgan pointed out in *TRAINS Magazine* (September 1962) that GE's Universal Line had a basic advantage over existing diesel-locomotive designs, because it was developed new, as opposed to suffering from the restraints of evolutionary development. Morgan credits the work of GE's John C. Aydelott, who coordinated the design of a new diesel-electric locomotive free from the prejudice of existing designs.

A potential disadvantage for GE in marketing its new diesel line was that its locomotives did not have a track record, while those of Alco and EMD were well known. Yet, General Electric was already well respected in the industry, and by taking time to work through engineering problems before selling its product, it hoped to deliver a well-designed machine that would deliver high output and good reliability while requiring only minimal maintenance.

New York Central U25B No. 2501 leads an eastbound train on the former Boston & Albany mainline at State Line Tunnel near Canaan, New York. General Electric diesels have been regularly used on the B&A route for the better part of half a century. *Jim Shaughnessy*

The engineer's controls on a new Union Pacific U25B, seen at Omaha, Nebraska, on September 11, 1962. *Union Pacific photo, John Gruber collection*

But a diesel-electric locomotive is not a simple machine. It uses many different components that must work together flawlessly in harsh operating conditions. Electro-Motive, with its mass-produced 567 series diesel, had set very high standards for reliability.

Working from its strengths, GE set out to build a machine with a much simpler electrical system. During the 1940s and 1950s, GE refined its already excellent traction motor designs while consolidating motor production facilities at its Erie, Pennsylvania, plant. GE also worked through the other elements of locomotive design, carefully choosing an appropriate prime mover and designing an effective air-flow and air-filtering system. Its Universal Line locomotives used far fewer components than competing models, and its railroad traction equipment was the most respected in the industry—even EMD traction motors emulated GE designs.

Cooper-Bessemer Engine

General Electric chose the Cooper-Bessemer V-type diesel as the basis for its new engine. In the early 1930s, the U.S. Navy had funded the research and development of diesel-engine design in order to procure better submarine propulsion.

Several different compact, high-output diesel designs resulted, including the Winton 201A two-cycle diesel, initially used by Electro-Motive; the Fairbanks-Morse opposed-piston engine; and the Cooper-Bessemer. Since the 1920s, General Electric had used a variety of diesel engines in its locomotives. It had used six-cylinder Cooper-Bessemers since the 1930s and was very familiar with the engine's performance. Morgan wrote in the September 1962 issue of *TRAINS Magazine* that GE examined some 46 different diesel engine designs before settling on the Cooper-Bessemer. While this may be true, it should be noted that the Cooper-Bessemer design had several fundamental similarities with Alco's engine designs, with which GE was also familiar. From an engineering perspective, it is often better to work with a familiar system than to attempt to design something completely new. Both the Cooper-Bessemers and the Alco engines were turbocharged, four-cycle V-types that operated at moderate rpm. By comparison, EMD's 567 engine was a supercharged two-cycle V-type diesel, and Fairbanks-Morse's engine was a two-cycle opposed-piston design.

General Electric contracted for the use of the Cooper-Bessemer design and expanded it into a larger, and thus more powerful, engine capable of substantially higher output than initially required. GE initially built locomotives with a maximum output of 2,000 horsepower and less but anticipated the need for a single-unit, single-engine locomotive that could develop as much as 4,000 horsepower. The engine was designed to meet these future needs, and it has proven to be a very good design. Today a 7FDL-16 produces 4,500 gross horsepower, and its inherent fuel economy advantage over EMD's two-cycle engines has given GE an edge in a highly competitive market.

In 1954, General Electric built four experimental diesel-electric locomotives that it used as testbeds to further road locomotive design. They were built in a traditional carbody style with two cab units and two boosters operated in A-B-B-A fashion. The cabs shared a styling treatment similar to that used by the Alco FA and GE electrics, such as the New Haven EP-5, built about the same time. One noticeable styling difference was the use of fluted sides. One cab and booster set used eight-cylinder C-B engines to generate 1,200 horsepower per unit; the other set used 12-cylinder C-B engines to develop 1,800 horsepower per unit. The entire four-unit set was initially numbered 750, painted

A Family Lines–painted U23B leads an eastbound CSX coal drag toward Allegheny Summit on the old Chesapeake & Ohio at Tuckahoe, West Virginia, on the bright clear morning of October 29, 1987. Family Lines was a pre–Seaboard System grouping of railroads that are now components of CSX. *J.D. Schmid*

in the Erie Railroad's blue-and-yellow livery, and operated on the Erie in freight service. In 1959, after GE was through experimenting, each of the four units was rebuilt with 12-cylinder C-B engines rated at 2,000 horsepower each and sold to Union Pacific.

Initially, General Electric was interested in expanding its export sales, and in 1956 debuted its new Universal Line for sales overseas. By the mid-1950s, the export market was larger than the waning domestic market. American manufacturers led the world in diesel-electric technology, and GE competed directly with EMD and Alco for lucrative export sales. EMD's exports included its G12, a 12-cylinder 1,200-horsepower model with a B-B wheel arrangement, and its G16, a 16-cylinder 1,600-horsepower locomotive with a C-C wheel arrangement. Alco offered its "World Locomotive" in various power configurations. GE's exports, like those of EMD and Alco, were designed to operate on significantly lighter track than American locomotives, and thus featured low axle weights. For this reason, six-axle models, both in A1A-A1A and C-C arrangements, were favored for export models. Additional axles spread out locomotive weight, keeping axle weight down. With the Universal Line, GE consolidated its export line and thus reduced engineering costs by producing standard models. In this respect, GE emulated one of the most successful elements of EMD's approach toward locomotive production.

At first, GE focused its exports toward developing nations that did not possess the ability to develop diesel-electric technology. In April 1959, GE advertised: "Because of their greater horsepower, tractive effort and versatility, GE diesel-electric locomotives *do more work faster*; fewer units are needed, and investment is kept to a minimum."

The Universal Line was built in several different models using FDL series Cooper-Bessemer diesels in 8- and 12-cylinder configurations. The FDL was an intercooled, turbocharged four-cycle diesel with dual camshafts and 9x10-1/2-inch (bore and stroke) cylinders, each with 667-ci displacement. The engine worked at 1,000 rpm. Cylinders and cylinder heads were individual assemblies, rather than single cast-iron blocks. Electrical components consisted of standard GE items, such as the 752 series traction motor.

Domestic Aspirations

General Electric quickly established its Universal Line as a practical export locomotive, enhancing the company's

Although only American railroads bought the pioneering U25B, the model was not unusual in Canada, as several American railroads operated some Canadian trackage. Yet this view on September 2, 1979, finds the type beyond its traditional territory; here, a matched set of three Conrail U25Bs is seen at Canadian Pacific's diesel shop at Agincourt Yard, near Toronto, Ontario. *J.D. Schmid*

credibility as a diesel-electric locomotive manufacturer, while giving it practical experience with locomotives in service. Working out design bugs takes time, and many problems only manifest themselves after many hours of rigorous service.

By the late 1950s, the American market was again ripening for increased sales. The September 1957 issue of *Diesel Railway Traction* reported that EMD general manager N.C. Dezendorf estimated that during the following five years, some 7,750 American diesel-electrics would be due for major rebuilding, and that both EMD and Alco were planning to accommodate such work. The builders also hoped that many railroads would take the opportunity to trade in diesels in the 1,350- to 1,500-horsepower range for new more powerful models.

Looking to capture its share of the expanding domestic market, General Electric advanced the FDL engine to

a 16-cylinder design in 1958. Then in 1959, it built two experimental 2,400-horsepower units. Louis Marre indicates in *Diesel Locomotives: The First 50 Years* that they were initially designated model XP24-1, indicating the type was intended as an eXPort model. Each of these high-hood road switchers was powered by an FDL-16 diesel rated at 2,400 horsepower. As with the 1954 experimentals, these locomotives tested on the Erie Railroad for the better part of a year, running approximately 100,000 miles in heavy service to give GE time to refine its designs and work out engineering problems. By 1960, GE was confident of its product and in April publicly announced its new domestic road locomotive, the U25B. Rated at 2,500 horsepower, the four-axle, four-motor U25B was the most powerful single-engine diesel-electric on the market at that time.

Only a few railroads attempted to extend the service lives of Universal Line locomotives. In 1977, Southern Pacific contracted Morrison-Knudsen of Boise, Idaho, to rebuild four U25Bs with Sulzer engines. They were re-designated TE70-4S models and painted in an attractive adaptation of SP's famous "Daylight" livery. Unfortunately, the units, nicknamed "popsicles" for their bright paint scheme, were not mechanically reliable, and they served out their days on the flat track of Oregon's Willamette Valley between Portland and Eugene. Here, two of the TE70-4S units lead 99 cars and a caboose westbound at Alford, Oregon, on the afternoon of May 25, 1979. *J.D. Schmid*

In the years after the Penn-Central merger, General Electric locomotives from the Pennsylvania, New York Central, and New Haven often shared assignments, along with newer GE units bought by PC. Unusual lash-ups were common sights, such as this set bringing a westbound freight around Horseshoe Curve in the summer of 1972. A former PRR U25C and a former NYC U30B are creeping up the grade, keeping the train moving as a crewmember attends to a failed GP40 in the consist. *Jeremy Plant*

79

Union Pacific's massive U50s were effectively two U25Bs on one frame, using a pair of 16-cylinder FDL engines to produce 5,000 horsepower. They rode on recycled B-B+B-B trucks from UP's 4,500-horsepower gas turbines. *Union Pacific photo, John Gruber collection*

Rather than introduce various models designed for different types of traffic, GE initially focused its domestic efforts on the U25B, the one model that it believed would be the best-selling type. To promote its U25B, GE built high-hood demonstrator sets that traveled from railroad to railroad as rolling examples. The U25B used an FDL-16 rated at 2,500 horsepower that was coupled to a GE GT-598 generator to provide DC current to four GE 752 traction motors, one powering each axle. In the standard configuration, the U25B used a 74:18 gear ratio designed for 65 miles per hour. David P. Morgan, in an article in the August 1960 *TRAINS Magazine*, indicated that GE would offer the U25B in a variety of different gear ratios, allowing maximum speeds between 65 and 92 miles per hour, a common practice that allowed railroads to obtain optimum performance for their desired service. While EMD locomotives used standard eight-notch control, the U25B came with a 16-notch control stand to allow for more precision control. The U25B measured 60 feet, 2 inches long; 14 feet, 7 inches tall; and

This view of the rising sun on September 14, 1977, was made from the rear cab window on the engineer's side of a Milwaukee Road U28B working with a freight toward Portage, Wisconsin. *John Gruber*

On June 2, 1973, Penn-Central U33B 2900 leads an Alco C628, GE U25B, and three EMD GP40s with the westbound TV-7 through Buffalo, New York. No. 2900, five years old in this view, was built for PC in 1968. *Doug Eisele*

The Burlington Northern merger of 1970 brought together an eclectic collection of locomotives, including a good sampling of GE units. Three six-axle "U-boats" of Northern Pacific and Burlington heritage—two U25Cs followed by a U33C—led a unit coal train bound for the powerplant at South Joliet, Illinois, under the semaphores at Joliet in early April 1971. The train is on the Gulf, Mobile & Ohio mainline, which ran parallel to the Santa Fe at this busy location. The GEs are renumbered for their new owner, but they still carry the colors of their predecessor lines. *Jeremy Plant*

10 feet, 3 inches wide, and weighed between 260,000 and 264,000 pounds. Using a 74:18 gear ratio, it delivered 81,000 pounds starting tractive effort. As with most diesel-electrics of the period, the U25B was intended to operate in multiple, thus allowing flexibility in the amount of power railroads assigned to trains.

The U25B demonstrators toured in 1961, and GE began accepting orders. The first sales were high-hood types, four to Union Pacific and eight to the Frisco. By the early 1960s, locomotives with low-short hoods (often described as a *low-nose*) were taking favor with American lines. This arrangement offered greater forward visibility and soon was standard with most new locomotives, including the

U25B from 1962 onward. This difference had little effect on locomotive performance, but made a significant difference in appearance. Southern Pacific was the first railroad to receive U25s with low-short hoods, two locomotives completed by GE in March 1962 and numbered 7500 and 7501. Ultimately, SP was one of the largest buyers of early GE products, purchasing 68 U25Bs.

General Electric's Universal Line earned the nickname "U-boats." *TRAINS Magazine*'s J. David Ingles has hinted that the first use of the moniker came from the Rock Island, one of GE's U25B customers. The nickname is an interpretation of GE's model designation system, which coincidentally mimicked that of the German navy's designation for its World War

The Michigan iron ore hauler Lake Superior & Ishpeming acquired a small fleet of former Burlington Northern U30Cs in 1989 and 1990 to replace older six-motor GE and Alco diesels in heavy service. On August 21, 1995, a pair of LS&I U30Cs wearing BN's Cascade Green livery crosses the Morgan Creek trestle at Eagle Mills, Michigan. *John Leopard*

In the 1980s, Guilford acquired a single former Detroit Edison U30C, which it numbered 663. It is seen leading DHT-4, an eastbound Sealand double-stack train, on the former Erie Railroad through the Canisteo River Valley near Cameron Mills, New York, at 12:30 P.M. on May 7, 1988. It was known colloquially as the "S.S. *Bickmore*" and for several years was the only six-motor GE on Guilford. It survived into the mid-1990s. *Brian Solomon*

II–era submarines, which were also known as U-boats. However, the designation may have also conveyed the claustrophobic confines of the GE's diesel cabs and low, narrow cab doors, which made them unpopular with some railroad crews. Another connotation may stem from GE's seemingly stealthy entry into the heavy locomotive market. To some observers, the U25B seemed to have appeared on-scene suddenly, as if it emerged from deep waters to torpedo the competition.

According to Marre's *Diesel Locomotives: The First 50 Years*, GE sold 476 U25Bs in a seven-year period ending in 1966, making the U25B one of GE's most successful single locomotive models up to that time. It had sold more of them in just a few years than its total production of mainline electrics for domestic railroads since 1900! More to the point, the U25B greatly outsold Alco's domestic offerings of the time. The combined domestic production totals of

General Electric's second round of double-diesels were U50Cs built for Union Pacific. They resembled the U50s of the early 1960s but featured the common C-C six-motor arrangement and were powered by a pair of 12-cylinder diesels. Wheeling past the sandstone cliffs beneath Windy Knoll, UP U50C No. 5026 leads an eastbound freight through Utah's Echo Canyon on June 12, 1974. *Tom Kline collection, photographer unknown*

General Electric U36B demonstrator locomotives are seen leading a Delaware & Hudson freight at Mechanicville, New York, in August 1968. This train is bound for Binghamton, New York; trailing the GEs are Erie-Lackawanna Alcos and EMDs. *Jim Shaughnessy*

Alco's 2,400-horsepower RS-27, 2,400-horsepower C-424, and 2,500-horsepower C-425—models that were comparable to the U25B—was less than 200 units. Even if Alco's 1,800-horsepower RS-36, 2,000-horsepower RS-32, and 2,000-horsepower C-420 were added in, Alco's four-motor domestic sales totals for the 1961–1966 period numbered less than 400 locomotives. GE had outdone its onetime partner in the road-locomotive business. GE's sales comparison with EMD, however, is less favorable. Between 1961 and 1963, EMD's 2,250-horsepower GP30 outsold GE's U25B better than 2 to 1; EMD's 2,500-horsepower GP35 sold nearly three times as many units as the U25B in less than three years. General Electric had a long way to go to match General Motors' sales, but its U25B gave it a solid foothold in the domestic market.

In 1963 GE brought out a six-motor version of the U25, designated U25C (C to indicate the three-axle trucks). Similar to the four-motor U25B in most respects, the U25C was designed for heavy freight service. It developed greater tractive effort at slow speed and was considered a specialized machine, as six-motor diesels were not yet standard road

power. GE sold just 113 units of the U25C in a little more than two years. During the 1960s, high-horsepower six-motors gained popularity, and by the early 1970s were more popular than four-motor types.

U28B and U28C

The U25B established GE as a heavy-diesel builder, and in a 15-year period it built more than 3,100 Universal series locomotives for American railroads. During the 1960s, competition resulted in a rapid increase in the maximum horsepower output of new locomotives, as well as in design improvements to improve reliability. At the end of 1965, GE boosted the output of its U-boat from 2,500 horsepower to 2,800 to match increases by EMD and Alco. The 2,800-horsepower U28B and U28C were produced for a little more than a year before GE boosted its standard output to 3,000 horsepower. The first U28Bs closely resembled U25Bs in that they used the same body style. Later U28Bs featured a different body style with a shorter nose section and did not feature a large step along the running boards toward the back of the locomotive.

Until the mid-1990s, Squaw Creek Coal used a pair of secondhand U33Cs to move unit coal trains in southern Indiana. The lead locomotive in this view is former Southern Railway No. 3809, originally constructed with a high nose. After Southern traded in 3809 to GE, it was rebuilt with a low nose and later resold to Squaw Creek in 1992. The trailing locomotive was formerly Burlington Northern 5752. These two, among the last U33Cs in regular service in the United States, are moving a coal train north of Yankeetown, Indiana, on October 26, 1994. Squaw Creek operated between the Ayrshire Mine near Booneville to docks on the Ohio River near Yankeetown, where the coal was transloaded onto barges. *John Leopard*

Santa Fe's 839 train is westbound at old Allard, a removed siding in the Tehachapis near Bealville, California, on August 18, 1979. On the lead are four 3,600-horsepower diesels: three GE U36Cs and an EMD SD45-2. The 839 (Barstow to Richmond) has just met Santa Fe's eastbound 901 (Richmond to Chicago) at the west switch of the siding at Bealville. The 901's caboose can be clearly seen above the top of the train. On the rear of 839, behind its caboose, is Santa Fe EMD SD40-2 No. 5045, being used as a manned helper. *J.D. Schmid*

During U28 production, GE implemented a significant electrical change by switching to an AC-DC transmission system. The new system used an alternator rather than a generator and employed silicon diodes to rectify alternating current to the direct current needed by traction motors. This reduced the number of components, decreased maintenance, and, most significantly, allowed for higher output to traction motors. To increase output, all three manufacturers made the switch to AC-DC transmission systems during the mid-1960s.

A passenger variation of the U28C, designated U28CG, was built for Santa Fe. Ten U28CGs utilizing steam generators to provide heat and electricity were painted in Santa Fe's warbonnet livery. Although geared for faster service, they closely resembled standard freight service U28Cs.

U30B and U30C

General Electric boosted its output again at the end of 1966, when it introduced the U30 models. As the model designation conveys, the U30 delivered 3,000 horsepower. Although, GE would introduce more powerful U-series locomotives, the U30B and U30C remained in continuous production for the better part of 10 years. The two models equaled the horsepower output of EMD's standard GP40 and SD40 models, which were among that builder's most popular models of the period. Nearly 600 U30Cs were sold to American railroads, making it the most popular of all U-series models.

A standard U30B measured 60 feet, 2 inches long, just over 15 feet tall, and slightly more than 10 feet, 3 inches wide. It weighed 254,800 pounds, used an FDL-16 engine

with an 81:22 gear ratio, and 40-inch wheels allowed it to deliver 54,100 pounds continuous tractive effort at 12 miles per hour. It was designed for 75-mile-per-hour operation and, like the U25B, was intended for fast freight work.

Technically, the U30C was largely the same as its four-motor counterpart but was slightly longer and heavier. It measured 67 feet, 3 inches long—the standard length for most GE six-motor U-series—and was slightly more than 15 feet, 4 inches tall. Its standard weight was 363,000 pounds and, using a 74:18 gear ratio, could deliver 90,600 pounds continuous tractive effort at 9.6 miles per hour. The U30C was designed for heavy freight operation and was often assigned to drag freights and mineral service. Burlington Northern operated the largest fleet, painted in the railroad's standard Cascade-green livery with white lettering and often assigned to Alliance, Nebraska, for Powder River coal trains originating in Wyoming. Santa Fe ordered a semi-streamlined cowl version of the U30C with a steam generator for passenger service.

In the mid-1970s, Amtrak ordered a 3,000-horsepower cowl type from GE, designated P30CH. These boxy machines measured 72 feet, 4 inches long and used a small auxiliary diesel engine and generator to provide head-end power rather than take power from the prime mover, as was done with other passenger diesel-electric types. The P30CHs were not a common sight, and for most of their service lives were assigned to Lorton, Virginia–Sanford, Florida, *Auto Train* service and to the *Sunset*, Amtrak's tri-weekly run over Southern Pacific's Sunset Route between New Orleans and Los Angeles.

High Horsepower U-Boats

General Electric met the demand for very high-horsepower diesels by increasing the output of its FDL diesel engine. Unlike EMD, which used a larger version of its 645 diesel to obtain greater output, GE made relatively minor adjustments to the FDL-16 engine, primarily adjusting the fuel rack to increase output and modifying the electrical and

Very few domestic Universal Line locomotives were regularly used in passenger service, making the fleet of U34CHs used on former Erie-Lackawanna lines radiating from Hoboken, New Jersey, especially unusual. New Jersey Transit U34CH No. 4172 sits below Hoboken Terminal's vintage Bush train sheds on October 11, 1992. *Brian Solomon*

At 6:33 A.M. on July 21, 1988, New Jersey Transit U34CH 4164, working in "push" mode, shoves its consist past Howells, New York, toward Hoboken. In regular operation, the U34CHs work in push-pull service, with the locomotives situated on the west end of passenger consists. *Brian Solomon*

cooling systems to accommodate greater output. The larger "bat-wing" radiators at the rear of the 3,300-horsepower U33B and U33C and the 3,600-horsepower U36B and U36C distinguish these models from 3,000-horsepower locomotives, but the basic layout of the locomotive and primary dimensions remained unchanged.

In addition, a U34CH model was built for passenger services on Erie-Lackawanna routes radiating from Hoboken Terminal in New Jersey. This was similar to the U36C, but diverted some output for head-end power. Marre indicates that the U34CH had 3,430 horsepower available for traction. They were paid for by the New Jersey Department of Transportation and delivered in a blue-and-silver variation of the Erie-Lackawanna paint scheme, featuring both the Erie-Lackawanna herald and the NJDOT logo. In the early 1980s, New Jersey Transit was created to operate New Jersey's suburban passenger trains, and many U34CHs were repainted in NJT's silver scheme. The U34CHs were regularly paired with lightweight Pullman-Standard coaches, and in their early years were occasionally used by Erie-Lackawanna in weekend freight service, when they were not required for passenger duties.

U23 and U18

Following the introduction of new high-output diesel-electrics, both EMD and GE brought out more moderately powered diesels. The primary application for high-output, four-motor diesels was hauling priority fast freights; they are unnecessary for slower trains such as local and branchline freights, and for lower-priority "drag" freights. Lower-output locomotives cost less to operate.

General Electric's moderately powered four-motor locomotive was the 2,250-horsepower U23B, powered by a 12-cylinder 7FDL engine. Externally, the U23B appears nearly identical to the more powerful U30B, but the catalog U23B weighed 242,000 pounds (11 tons less than the U30B) and developed 57,200 pounds continuous tractive effort at 11.9 miles per hour. Commercially, the U23B was one of GE's most successful Universal types—465 were sold for North American service, nearly as many as the U25B—and it remained in regular production until 1977. The basis for the successful B23-7 design, the U23B was also one of the longest surviving U-boats, with some models serving for more than 25 years.

The U23C was built for specialized service. Like the U23B, this locomotive used a 12-cylinder 7FDL to produce 2,250 horsepower, but developed considerably more tractive effort. Using the 74:18 gear ratio, a U23C developed 85,800 pounds at 7.3 miles per hour. Railroads such as Penn-Central used them for heavy yard work, where high tractive effort at slow speeds was needed, and a high-output diesel engine would have been unnecessary. The U23C shared common dimensions with the U30C, but with standard options weighed slightly less. Although the type remained in GE's catalog for a number of years, just over 50 were built for domestic purposes between 1968 and 1970, making it one of the more unusual GE types.

Another fairly unusual model was the low-output U18B, which used an eight-cylinder 7FDL to produce 1,800 horsepower. Seaboard Coast Line and Maine Central (MEC) were the primary domestic buyers. Some U18s made use of recycled components from old EMD models traded in to GE, and many U18Bs rode on EMD's Blomberg trucks, as did some other GE four-motor types built during the same

Delaware & Hudson U30Cs are seen at Mohawk Yard in Glenview, New York, just across the river from Schenectady. In the late 1970s, D&H sold its 12 U30Cs for operation in Mexico. *Jim Shaughnessy*

period. Bought to replace Maine Central's aging Alco road switchers, the U18Bs were delivered on the eve of the American bicentennial and thus designated as the railroad's "Independence Class." They were painted in an attractive bright yellow livery with a green stripe and adorned with large, stylized American eagles on the nose. Each locomotive was named in tribute to Revolutionary War heroes and locations. Maine Central assigned its U18Bs to road freights, and often used them on its legendary Mountain Division that connected Portland, Maine, to St. Johnsbury, Vermont, crossing over New Hampshire's Crawford Notch. Some of MEC's U18Bs remained in service for more than 25 years and later wore the gray-and-orange paint of MEC's owner, Guilford, which also operated the Boston & Maine (and the Delaware & Hudson from 1984 to 1988).

While the U18B was the lowest-rated domestic Universal model and was only built between 1973 and 1976, General Electric had offered a variety of low-output models for export after the 1950s. The U17B, for example, used an eight-cylinder 7FDL engine, but was only 46 feet, 4-1/2 inches long (almost 8 feet shorter than the U18B) and weighed just 164,000 pounds, in order to accommodate lines with very low axle weights. General Electric's low-output export C-C Universal models, such as the 1,550-horsepower U15C and the 1,820-horsepower U18C, were also much lighter than domestic locomotives. They were offered in a variety of different gauges and built to a substantially lower profile, measuring just under 12 feet, 6 inches tall. The least powerful Universal Line exports were powered by Caterpillar diesels instead of Cooper-Bessemer FDL engines.

The U10B—one of several models that remained in GE's export catalog for years after domestic production had switched to the Dash-7 line—used a Caterpillar D379 engine to produce 1,050 gross horsepower with 950 available for traction. Its electrical transmission system was of a fairly simple direct current design and employed GE's GT 602 generator and GE761 traction motors.

U50

Union Pacific was the first railroad to purchase the U25B, but it only operated a relatively small fleet of 16. Yet, Union Pacific was impressed with GE's road diesel and prompted the builder for something more powerful. Greg McDonnell relates that UP's motive power chief, David S. Neuhart, convinced GE, as well as EMD and Alco, to develop massive double-diesel types. In GE's case, UP wanted to replace its first-generation turbines. What GE came up with was effectively a double U25 that incorporated recycled components from the turbines, including Association of American

Above: On the first day of winter 1979, Maine Central U18B No. 406 leads the eastbound YR-1 over the Mountain Division at Crawford Notch. Maine Central was one of the few railroads to purchase GE's 1,800-horsepower U18B. *Jim Shaughnessy*

Right: In 1969 the Delaware & Hudson purchased 16 U23Bs, the first and only four-axle GE units on the railroad. Originally numbered 301 through 316, they were renumbered 2301 through 2316 in 1971. In October 1974, during peak autumn color, a matched set of four clean U23Bs slowly grinds up Kelley's Grade (0.8 percent) at Delanson, New York, on the line from Schenectady. The train has just picked up a block of heavy ore cars at Mohawk Yard and is being assisted by another U23B and an Alco RS11 working as a helper at the rear of the train. *Jeremy Plant*

Railroads (AAR) Type B trucks in the unusual B-B+B-B arrangement. The U50s were 83 feet, 6 inches long, weighed 558,000 pounds, and used a pair of 7FDL-16 diesels to produce 5,000 horsepower. The cab rode higher than on other diesel-electric types and featured a distinctive front end with a much smaller nose section than was typical of American diesels. Union Pacific took delivery of 23 U50s between 1963 and 1965. Southern Pacific, which at the time was also experimenting with high-output imported Krauss-Maffei diesel-hydraulics, bought three U50s that were built in spring 1964. They featured minor differences from the UP's, weighing about 3,000 pounds less and featuring doors on the nose section and variations in their braking and wheel slip–control equipment. SP based its U50s at Taylor Yard in Los Angeles and often assigned them to Sunset Route services. Both UP and SP regularly used U50s in combination with other locomotives, including U25Bs.

In the late 1960s, Union Pacific encouraged further development of double-diesel types. GE answered with a new variation of the U50 type that rode on C-C trucks from the 8,500-horsepower turbines and were appropriately designated U50Cs. Union Pacific bought the entire production run of 40 built between 1969 and 1971. In addition to different trucks, these later U50s featured several other significant differences from the first batch of U50s. Advances in the FDL engine design permitted GE to use a pair of 12-cylinder engines to develop 5,000 horsepower. As a result, the U50C was shorter and lighter, measuring 79 feet long and weighing 141,000 pounds less than the U50 type. Another change was the use of aluminum wiring, which unfortunately resulted in serious electrical difficulties. McDonnell indicates that several U50Cs suffered fires that caused their premature retirement.

Maine Central U18Bs are seen at Bangor, Maine, on a cold winter night, February 17, 1976. Maine Central regularly assigned its U18Bs to road freights, working them in consists with the railroad's EMDs and Alcos. *Don Marson*

DASH-7

From the beginning, American railroad locomotive purchases have followed a cyclical pattern, typically providing builders with a feast-or-famine marketplace. When the economy is doing well and traffic is up, railroads are hungry for new power and place large orders for new motive power; when economic conditions cool, new locomotive orders drop off precipitously. Peak times result in the largest numbers of new locomotives, but traditionally the times of the poorest locomotive sales have resulted in the most significant developments in locomotive technology. Smart builders wait out lean years by planning for the next boom. During times of low production, builders have the opportunity to experiment and test new concepts, advance new technology, and design new locomotives with minimal pressure from the market. The Great Depression, for example, saw the advancement of the diesel-electric locomotive, while the economic slowdown of the late 1950s and early 1960s, which coincided with the completion of dieselization, resulted in the development of substantially more powerful diesel-electrics and gave GE the opportunity to enter the road-diesel market.

The mid-1970s saw another period of slow economic activity. An article by Kenneth Ellswoth in the January 31, 1977, issue of *Railway Age* summed up the climate in its opening sentence: "Final returns aren't in yet, but it looks as if 1976 was the worst year since 1961 for the installation of new locomotives by the railroads."

Opposite: New England–based Providence & Worcester was one of the few smaller railroads that bought new GE locomotives. It ordered a single B23-7, No. 2201, which was delivered with an expanded lighting package that included an oscillating headlight. In later years, P&W acquired a sizable fleet of secondhand GEs, including U23Bs, B30-7ABs, and Super 7s. On December 6, 1993, P&W B23-7 No. 2202 and a U23B lead a freight at Old Saybrook, Connecticut. *Brian Solomon*

General Electric has historically had the foresight to use slow periods to great advantage. In recent decades, every economic recession has allowed GE to advance its designs and produce even better machines that have permitted the company to capture greater shares of the domestic locomotive market.

The recession of the mid-1970s came with its share of special circumstances. The fuel crisis of 1973 and 1974 had driven up the price of crude oil and consequentially the price of diesel fuel. While fuel efficiency had always been a locomotive design concern, fuel efficiency suddenly became a major issue. The fuel crisis gave GE a distinct market advantage over EMD, because General Electric's four-cycle 7FDL diesel engine is inherently more fuel-efficient than EMD's two-cycle 645 design. GE hoped to play this design strength to its advantage and use it to gain market share. However, as Alco had found out a decade earlier, fuel efficiency alone does not sell locomotives. Despite Alco's advertisements and demonstrations of better fuel economy, EMD continued to dominate the locomotive market, as a result of its higher reliability and lower maintenance costs—railroads wanted fuel efficiency combined with high reliability.

During the 1960s and early 1970s, General Electric's Universal Line captured a significant share of the new locomotive market, and in the mid-1970s GE sought to improve its reputation for lower reliability than comparable EMD products. By addressing specific railroad concerns and stressing its locomotives' superior fuel consumption, GE captured a greater share of the market when the economy picked up at the end of the decade. According to period advertisements and articles in *Railway Age*, GE sought advice from the railroads on how to improve locomotive design for its "New Series" of locomotive. GE wasn't just looking to spiff up its Universal Line, but to debut a whole new line. One ad in a 1976 *Railway Age* read:

"Early in 1974, General Electric began interviewing top railroad mechanical officers to seek an answer to an innovative question: given the opportunity, how would railroads themselves design a better locomotive?

"The result was an evolutionary program, which led to 58 design and component advances. An additional 20 have also become standard on the New Series locomotive."

General Electric introduced its "New Series" of locomotives in 1977. This line improved upon the Universal Line and allowed the company to gain market share. Three Conrail C30-7As are seen against the setting sun at Palmer, Massachusetts, on September 30, 1991. *Brian Solomon*

Three Conrail B23-7s lead a freight at CP Draw in Buffalo, New York, on April 22, 1989. GE's B23-7 was a moderately powerful model designed for road and switching work. Railroads such as Conrail used them as general workhorse locomotives, assigning them to yards, local freights, and road freights, as needed. Conrail's B23-7s were equipped with Association of American Railroad (AAR) trucks, a traditional design used on a great many models over the years.
Brian Solomon

The basics behind General Electric's new locomotive line remained the same: They used the 7FDL diesel—the latest variation of the 752 traction motor—and other primary components that had proven their reliability. GE avoided major design changes that would introduce a host of new primary components, which railroads may have avoided until they were proven. While the new locomotives retained their fundamental components, GE implemented numerous small changes to produce a more refined, higher-quality machine that would better suit the everyday needs of railroads. Among these improvements was a redesigned engineer's cab that followed Association of American Railroads (AAR) guidelines. The new cab featured a standard location for the conductor's emergency brake valve release, a more convenient toilet, Lexan (safety glass) on the side windows, better sun visors, better access to locomotive number lights and headlights, and hinge guards on the doors. The electrical compartment arrangement was improved by separating the high-voltage and low-voltage equipment. A walk-in low-voltage compartment, situated behind the engineer's cab, featured a user-friendly control arrangement and diagnostic equipment that made the correction of malfunctions simpler and easier. High-voltage electrical control equipment was located in cabinets below the cab. Other improvements included a better arrangement of auxiliary equipment such as the air compressor, water tank, and oil filters at the back of the locomotive. Some equipment, such as blowers, that were formerly located at the front of the locomotive were relocated to the back to accommodate the cab rearrangement. On Universal Line locomotives, the air compressor, used to generate air for the air brake, had been located in the radiator compartment. To minimize the compressor's exposure to oil and oil vapors, and to ensure that it was properly ventilated, it was relocated to a sealed-off section of the engine room on the New Series locomotives.

The changes paid off—GE soon enjoyed increased sales and an improved reputation. The crowning achievement of this investment occurred in 1983 when General Electric outsold EMD for the first time.

Dash-7 Designations and Details

Initially, GE called its new line the "New Series." However, later company documents referred to the post–Universal Line locomotives as the "Series-7." Since the introduction

of the DASH 8 line in the mid-1980s, the Series-7 locomotives have been commonly referred to as "Dash-7s," referring to the revised designation system that GE introduced with the "New Series." In this revised nomenclature, the first letter in the model name was either a B or a C to signify the number of axles/motors (B=four axles/four motors and C=six axles/six motors). The letter was followed by a two-digit number to identify the horsepower, then a dash, and finally the number 7 to indicate that the locomotive line was introduced in 1977. Thus, a six-axle 3,000-horsepower road switcher described in the Universal Line as a U30C was designated a C30-7.

Although GE had altered the platform somewhat to provide a better arrangement of essential locomotive systems, the outward appearance of the Dash-7 closely resembled Universal Line locomotives. For locomotive watchers, one of

the few spotting differences that clearly identifies Dash-7 models is a subtle step in the width of the hood toward the rear of the locomotive. GE's Universal Line locomotive hoods featured a smoother profile between the engine cab and the radiator cab.

The Dash-7 Catalog

General Electric initially offered its Dash-7 series in about a dozen different model configurations that ranged in output from 1,800 to 3,600 horsepower and came in four-motor/four-axle and six-motor/six-axle arrangements. Of these models, only the B23-7, B30-7, B36-7, C30-7, and C36-7 were built for domestic use. Models like the B18-7, C23-7, and C28-7, which corresponded to similar Universal Line locomotives, as well as to comparable EMD products, were listed in GE's catalog but never constructed for use in

Left: Sometimes a photographer just gets lucky! On October 28, 1992, an eastbound CSX mixed freight led by a pair of DASH 8-40Cs descending Sand Patch meets a westbound intermodal train charging upgrade through the Falls Cut Tunnel (Pennsylvania) with a set of four B36-7s. Seaboard System, a component of CSX, received its fleet of B36-7s from GE in 1985. *Brian Solomon*

Below: Four CSX B36-7s lead a westbound intermodal train west of Meyersdale, Pennsylvania, on the afternoon of October 22, 1992. *Brian Solomon*

the United States. The C23-7, for example, would have been a six-motor 2,250-horsepower locomotive powered by a 12-cylinder 7FDL diesel.

Typical Universal Line locomotives used GE 7FDL diesels in either 12- or 16-cylinder configurations depending on the locomotive model. All domestic Dash-7 locomotives used the latest versions of the proven GE 752 traction motors. Forty-inch driving wheels were standard with most domestic Dash-7s.

Over the course of Dash-7 production, GE implemented a variety of additional improvements intended to further boost reliability and result in better fuel efficiency. For example, later Dash-7s were equipped with an eddy-current clutch (an electromagnetic clutch activated electrically) to operate the radiator fan. On previous locomotives, the radiator fan was mechanically driven from the engine and therefore operated continuously whether or not the engine (or, more specifically, the radiators) needed cooling. Additional fuel-saving features were the introduction of a new fuel injection pump, known as the 18-millimeter double-helix design (describing the diameter of the pump plunger)

Right: Conrail regularly assigned high-horsepower, four-motor locomotives to its fast intermodal trains. In September 1988, three B36-7s race eastward near School Road in Batavia, New York, along the old New York Central mainline, the route of the famous *20th Century Limited.* Brian Solomon

Below: A westbound Conrail "Trailvan" crosses a small deck bridge on the former New York Central Water Level Route near Palmyra, New York, in May 1989. Conrail had a fleet of 60 GE B36-7s, numbered 5000 to 5059. They were equipped with GE's "floating bolster" trucks, designed for high adhesion. Brian Solomon

to supplant an earlier model. The new pump varied fuel injection timing with the quantity of fuel injected and thus lowered fuel consumption when the locomotive was operating in the lower throttle positions.

General Electric Dash-7 production saw other changes that were not a direct result of the new line but reflected other contemporary changes in the industry. In the late 1970s, because locomotives needed to comply with more stringent federal sound emissions standards, later Dash-7s were equipped with more effective engine mufflers. This is the reason later Dash-7s sound less impressive than earlier GE models—instead of a pronounced, throaty chugging sound, muffler-equipped models emit a softer tone. To reduce smoke emissions and improve fuel economy, GE also introduced a modified throttle position arrangement described as the "skip three, double seven" schedule. This refers to the traditional eight-position AAR throttle, wherein position one is the lowest and position eight is the highest.

"Skip three, double seven" revised the diesel engine speed and load schedule, running it at higher crankshaft speeds than in the earlier AAR schedule.

An external change was the loss of the extra side windows in the locomotive cab. Traditionally, GE models featured two smaller, unopenable windows bracketing the main window on the side of the cab. According to Union Pacific locomotive historian Don Strack, the introduction of more expensive shatterproof Lexan glass discouraged railroads from spending extra money, leading to the discontinuation of side windows. In some Dash-7 models, the spaces for these windows remained in the cab but were covered with sheet metal. Later models didn't provide a space for the extra windows.

B23-7

This intermediate output B23-7 was basically an improved version of the U23B and was intended for the same type of

service. Slightly longer than the U23B, it measured 62 feet, 2 inches and used a 12-cylinder 7FDL diesel that produced 2,250 horsepower. The typical B23-7 weighed 280,000 pounds and produced 70,000 pounds starting tractive effort (based on 25 percent adhesion). The model was offered with three different gear ratios, but the 83:20 ratio designed for 70 miles per hour was probably the most common. This gearing allowed the locomotive to deliver 63,250 pounds continuous tractive effort at 10.7 miles per hour.

The B23-7 was built with several different types of trucks, depending on customer preference. Some locomotives, such as those ordered by Conrail, used AAR's Type B truck; others, such as those used by the Norfolk Southern predecessor Southern Railway, employed GE's floating bolster truck; a third option was recycled EMD Blomberg trucks that came in with EMD trade-ins. Most B23-7s were

Southern Railway always bought road switchers with high-short hoods, and continued to order new locomotives with this arrangement until years after most other railroads switched to the low-short hood configuration. High-hood Southern B23-7 No. 3972 leads train 173 at Ruffin, North Carolina, in the autumn of 1986. *Doug Koontz*

Among the more unusual domestic GE models were 10 BQ23-7s built for CSX predecessor Family Lines. These locomotives featured "Quarters Cabs" designed to accommodate a larger crew and allow for some of the first caboose-less operations. Family Lines BQ23-7 No. 5134 leads the Ringling Brothers Barnum & Bailey Circus train at Wingate, North Carolina, on March 3, 1983. *Doug Koontz*

The sun momentarily pierces the cloud cover over Buffalo, New York, on March 19, 1989, to reveal a pair of Seaboard System–painted C30-7s paused with a Detroit-Buffalo freight at CP 437 in front of the abandoned Buffalo Terminal. At this time, CSX regularly operated its Detroit-Buffalo freight via Ontario. The once-magnificent Buffalo Terminal building was designed by Fellheimer and Wagner, and was inspired in part by the main station in Helsinki, Finland. *Brian Solomon*

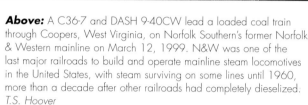

ordered with low-short hoods, but Southern Railway ordered the model with high-short hoods. An unusual variation of the model was the BQ23-7, 10 of which were ordered by Family Lines. This model featured a large boxy cab designed to accommodate a three-man crew. The BQ23-7 was a temporary solution offered by the railroad in the late 1970s, when the line was trying to get rid of its cabooses.

According to figures published by Louis A. Marre and Paul K. Withers in *The Contemporary Diesel Spotter's Guide*, 446 B23-7s (including the BQ23-7s) were built for North American service. This figure includes a large order of locomotives assembled by GE's Brazilian affiliate for the National Railways of Mexico.

B30-7 and B36-7

These high-horsepower Dash-7 models corresponded to the Universal Line U30B and U36B, and like those locomotives were intended for high-priority, fast freight services, such as intermodal trains. In many respects, these models closely resembled the B23-7 except for minor variations in external vents on the sides of the locomotives. The primary difference was that they were powered by a 16-cylinder 7FDL diesel rated at 3,000 or 3,600 horsepower for the B30-7 and B36-7, respectively. The combined production total of these two models was 421, just under that for the domestic production of B23-7s.

These locomotives were the hot rods of the industry when they were new, and they were assigned to some of the fastest trains in the country. Conrail and Santa Fe used them to haul their transcontinental piggyback trains, such as the TVLA/QNYLA, which ran from the New York area to Los Angeles on an expedited schedule. Santa Fe was legendary for its fast freights operating on passenger-train-like schedules, some of which ran from Chicago to Los Angeles in just 52 hours. Likewise, Southern Pacific and its affiliate, Cotton Belt, used its B30-7s and B36-7s on the ultra-hot *Blue Streak* and *Memphis Blue Streak* intermodal runs. The *Blue Streak* was originally conceived as a fast less-than-carload (LCL) train connecting St. Louis and Texas and was intended to help SP/Cotton Belt to win back business lost to trucks during the 1920s. By the late 1970s this train had become SP's premier freight and one of the best-known freight trains in America.

C30-7

During the 1970s and early 1980s, the best-selling locomotive types were 3,000-horsepower six-motor machines. While EMD's SD40/SD40-2 types were by far the most numerous, General Electric sold a respectable number of its U30C, and later its C30-7. According to *The Contemporary Diesel Spotter's Guide*, GE built more than 1,100 C30-7s for North American service, making it GE's best-selling locomotive up to that time. Some were sold to Mexico as kits and assembled there. Burlington Northern, Union Pacific, and Norfolk Southern, and CSX predecessors bought large numbers of C30-7s for heavy freight service, commonly using them on unit coal trains. Moving slow-speed heavy trains was one of the strengths of GE's locomotive design and the C30-7s were known for their excellent lugging abilities. A standard C30-7 was powered by a 16-cylinder 7FDL diesel that produced 3,000 horsepower. Fully loaded, a typical C30-7 weighed 420,000 pounds and could deliver 105,000 pounds starting tractive effort (assuming dry rail with a 25 percent factor of adhesion). In later years, Union Pacific listed its C30-7s as weighing 395,000 pounds, more than 12 tons less than GE's specifications for a new locomotive. Assuming standard weight, 40-inch wheels, and 70-mile-per-hour gearing using an 83:20 ratio, a C30-7 would deliver 96,900 pounds continuous tractive effort at 8.8 miles per hour. As with other GE six-motor diesels, the C30-7 rode on a 67-foot, 3-inch platform.

C36-7

The most powerful locomotive in General Electrics' Dash-7 line was its C36-7. Significant technological changes were implemented during the production run to make later C36-7s near cousins of GE's DASH 8 locomotives. The C36-7 was introduced in 1978 as a 3,600-horsepower model, but later examples featured enhanced engine output rated at 3,750 horsepower. The C36-7 uses virtually identical mechanical equipment as the C30-7; the models employ the same platform, the FDL diesel engine, and other primary components. GE obtained greater output from the engine through adjustments to the fuel rack and related systems.

GE C36-7s built after 1983 incorporated sophisticated electronic control systems that had been tested on pre-production DASH 8 locomotives and were actually built alongside the classic DASH 8 models. Later C36-7s provided greater tractive effort because of improved adhesion made possible by GE's SENTRY adhesion control system. According to GE promotional literature, the SENTRY system used traction-motor shaft speed sensors in place of older axle-mounted systems. The motor shaft sensors were as much as six times more sensitive to speed fluctuations, allowing for more detailed corrections to wheel slip and a better application of sand to the rail. Depending on the severity of wheel slip, the SENTRY system would automatically sand the rail

Continued on page 108

In 1985, Union Pacific's Missouri Pacific component took delivery of hybrid C36-7s that incorporated some DASH 8 technology and were rated at 3,750 horsepower instead of the lower 3,600 rating assigned to early C36-7 models. This view features 9016 at North Platte, Nebraska, in September 1989. Notice the DASH 8–style dynamic-brake grids on the hump-like box behind the cab. In 2002, some of these locomotives were rebuilt and re-gauged by GE for service in Estonia. *Brian Solomon*

GE IN ESTONIA

It is July 2002. Sitting among a host of curious-looking, Russian-built M62 diesels is a pair of glistening burgundy-and-gold GE C36-7s waiting to head east on a 60-car freight. This is a long way from North Platte; we're in Tallinn, Estonia—what are big GEs doing here?

Following the dissolution of the Soviet Union, the three Baltic States—Estonia, Latvia, and Lithuania—regained their independence. In the decade that followed, Estonia has been one of the most progressive former Soviet states, adopting Western-style business practices, while preening for inclusion in an expanded European Union. Part of this process has led to the sectorization and semi-privatization of the national railway network. The Estonian National Railway (known locally as Eesti Raudtee, or by its initials EVR) is the semiprivate company responsible for moving freight; EVR is a major outlet for Russian freight traffic. In 2001, a consortium of American, British, and Estonian interests known as Baltic Rail Services purchased a majority interest in EVR. Leading this transnational effort is American Ed Burkhardt of Rail World. Burkhardt is well known and respected in both American and international circles for his ability to transform freight railroads. In the 1980s and 1990s, the recently formed Wisconsin Central flourished under his leadership.

To make the Estonian effort succeed, Burkhardt and his team needed to find ways to reduce operating expenses in order to make EVR more profitable. By American standards, the railway has an excellent market share and moves a great volume of

In 2002, General Electric rebuilt former Union Pacific C36-7s for service on Estonian Railways. These locomotives received the modified designation C36-7i. In order to accommodate the broader gauge used in Estonia, GE cast new trucks for 5-foot gauge. *Brian Solomon*

traffic, primarily Russian oil. EVR's trains are heavy by European standards and operate on frequent headways. However, EVR's motive power was a collection of inefficient and unreliable Soviet-era diesels. After surveying various options to buy new and used diesels, EVR turned to General Electric to supply a fleet of secondhand motive power. GE offered refurbished units at a very good price, and EVR agreed to purchase 55 former Union Pacific (originally Missouri Pacific) C36-7s and 19 former Conrail C30-7As.

After more than 16 years of hauling Union Pacific freight across the mountains, plains, and deserts of the American West, UP's C36-7s had nearly reached the end of their natural service lives. Yet, GE and Burkhardt's team at EVR felt that with some overhaul and modifications, they were ideally suited for heavy service in Estonia. General Electric overhauled and re-gauged the units; because Estonian railways use the Russian 5-foot track gauge, new trucks were cast. Other modifications included equipping them with Russian-style SA3 knuckle couplers and fitting class lamps on the nose sections. To improve performance and reliability, the locomotives were equipped with GE's Bright Star high-adhesion computer system, which maximizes output while protecting electrical equipment from overloading. The refurbished GEs were painted in Burkhardt's preferred livery colors of burgundy and gold, similar to those he had used on Wisconsin Central and the British-based freight operation, the English-Welsh-Scottish Railway. The EVR logo is a variation of the "wheel with

reliable and less maintenance intensive than the Russian diesels that EVR management experts will be able to drastically curtail shop expenses while improving locomotive productivity and overall efficiency. A single C36-7i can handle a 6,700-ton train of Russian oil from the Russian frontier to the port of Tallinn, replacing a set of semi-permanently coupled 2M62 diesels. Typically, EVR freights had been limited to about 60 cars, but with the GEs, EVR has experimented with running trains up to 90 cars long, hauled by just two C36-7is.

GE has impressed and astounded Estonian railroaders and these C36-7is have performed better than anything that has ever operated here before.

Eesti Raudtee (Estonian Railways) C36-7i Nos. 1509 and 1520 were rebuilt by General Electric in May 2002. They are seen here shortly after entering service in Estonia, at the shops in Tallinn. Eesti Raudtee No. 1509 began service as a Missouri Pacific (Union Pacific) locomotive. To the right of the GEs is a Russian-built M62 diesel-electric of the type the C36-7s were bought to replace. *Brian Solomon*

In Estonia, freight trains are typically limited to 60 cars and weigh about 5,600 U.S. tons. While relatively small compared to some American freights, they are still much heavier than those operated in Western Europe. On July 25, 2002, a pair of freshly rebuilt GE C36-7s leads a westbound Eesti Raudtee freight from Narva (on the border with Russia) to Tallinn, Estonia. *Brian Solomon*

wings" theme that is found throughout railways in Eastern Europe, from Austria to Russia.

A variety of technical and political hurdles needed to be overcome before the American GEs could be operated in Estonia. The refurbished C36-7s (now designated C36-7i) were shipped by boat to Tallinn starting in May 2002. By July, they were hauling freight to and from the Russian frontier. The C36-7s represent a technological revolution on Estonian rails. Built new in 1985, the same time as many of the M62s they were bought to replace, they are having the same effect on Estonian motive power that the first mass-produced diesels—EMD F-units and Alco-GE FAs—had on steam power in America. The GEs are so much more

Continued from page 105

Union Pacific C36-7 No. 9006 leads an empty potash train at the base of Telocassset Hill east of Union Junction, Oregon, at 4:25 p.m. on June 13, 1993. The Missouri Pacific C36-7s were re-lettered for Union Pacific in the late 1980s. *Brian Solomon*

Class H insulation and other design refinements allowed GE to wrap more copper on the armature coils and obtain a 6 percent increase in motor rating (presumably over the GE 752E8 motor, a previous design that GE used as a basis for comparison). To minimize power losses attributed to eddy currents, motor armature coils used a pair of conductors in parallel in place of a single conductor. Additional motor improvements included a better gear-case design and better insulation on motor field coils intended to give better moisture resistance and superior performance in high temperatures.

General Electric built 129 C36-7s between 1978 and 1985 for North American service. Many of these machines were the later, more powerful models with SENTRY adhesion control. These transitional models were some of the first to employ microprocessor controls.

General Electric specifications for the late-era C36-7 indicate a fully loaded locomotive weighing 420,000 pounds could deliver 105,000 pounds starting tractive effort (based on 25 percent adhesion), the same as the C30-7. However, with 70-mile-per-hour 83:20 gearing and 40-inch wheels, a C36-7 could deliver 96,900 pounds at 11 miles per hour, rather than 8.8 miles per hour as with a C30-7. In other words, the C36-7 could move the same tonnage continuously at greater speeds.

Some of the most advanced C36-7s were an order of 60 built for the Missouri Pacific in 1985. By that time, MoPac had become a part of the Union Pacific system, as a result of the 1981 Union Pacific–Missouri Pacific–Western Pacific merger. These big GEs were delivered in Union Pacific paint with Missouri Pacific lettering, but were generally assigned to road service all across the Union Pacific system. Don Strack indicates that in the late 1980s, the C36-7s were re-lettered for Union Pacific.

Among the microprocessor advances used on these locomotives was what GE described as a Motor Thermal Protection panel, which electronically monitored the conditions of the traction motors while calculating the effects of ambient temperature and automatically regulating the current supplied to them to avoid damage from overloading. On older locomotives, the engineer needed to watch the ammeter on the control stand to monitor traction motor conditions and use personal judgment when working in short time ratings. The Motor Thermal Protection

and make small, calculated reductions to motor output. The system was specially designed to aid locomotive traction in poor weather conditions.

Another improvement related to the SENTRY system was the GE 752AH traction motor, the latest variation of the traditional 752 family of motors. In its promotional literature, GE stated the GE 752AH has a higher continuous current rating than earlier 752 motors. Using advanced

system was a real advantage for Union Pacific, which operates trains in some the most extreme weather conditions in North America.

12-Cylinder Economy

In the early 1980s, General Electric offered 3,000-horsepower models with a 12-cylinder 7FDL diesel in place of a 16-cylinder engine. These locomotives received an "A"designation after their normal model number to distinguish them from ordinary 16-cylinder models. The theory behind the 12-cylinder models was that better fuel economy could be obtained by employing an engine with fewer cylinders. Since the output of the 7FDL diesel had been boosted dra-

matically since its introduction, GE found it could easily push a 12-cylinder design to produce 3,000 horsepower. Between 1980 and 1983, GE produced several variations of B30-7As in a production run totaling just over 200 units. Among these were 120 cabless B30-7ABs built for Burlington Northern in 1982 and 1983. Although BN didn't order similar Dash-7 models with cabs, in later years it often operated these "B-units" with its LMX GE B39-8 lease fleet, running them in A-B and A-B-A sets.

In 1984, Conrail ordered a fleet of 50 C30-7As that used 12-cylinder engines. Numbered 6550 to 6599, these Dash-7s were intended for high-tractive-effort, moderate-speed applications where good fuel efficiency

In 1984, GE built 50 C30-7As for Conrail. The C30-7A uses a 12-cylinder 7FDL diesel instead of the 16-cylinder engine used in standard C30-7s. At 10:10 A.M. on June 18, 1988, Conrail TV-9 (Boston-to-Chicago Trailvan), led by C30-7A and two C32-8s, overtakes a laden ballast train powered by three C30-7As at Chatham Center, New York, on the former Boston & Albany mainline. *Brian Solomon*

Northbound Alberta RailNet (ARN) train No. 458 is seen along the Wildhay River Valley on September 21, 2002. ARN operates on former CN and Northern Alberta Railway trackage, using a fleet of secondhand four- and six-axle GEs to haul coal. These two former Norfolk & Western C30-7s are leading a former Santa Fe SF30C. Other locomotives in the ARN fleet were originally built for the Louisville & Nashville, Frisco, and Southern. Most are leased from the Livingston (Montana) Rebuild Center. *John Leopard*

Conrail had one of the most diverse fleets of General Electric locomotives, variously consisting of more than 20 different models. Its 25 C36-7s, built in 1985, operated in the railroad's general road pool. The first in the series was locomotive 6620 (numbered after the C32-8s) seen here at Frontier Yard, Buffalo, New York, in 1988. *Brian Solomon*

was a significant objective. They were frequently assigned to Selkirk Yard, south of Albany, New York, for service on the rugged Boston Line, the former Boston & Albany mainline. In their early years, the C30-7As were typically assigned in sets of three and sometimes mixed with the similarly powered C32-8 prototypes (see Chapter 6). In later years, it was more typical for Conrail to operate the C30-7As in sets of four and to occasionally mix them with other modern GE six-motor types.

C36-7s for Export

By far the largest order for C36-7s was for an export variety built during the early and mid-1980s for operation in China. At the time, the first Chinese order was the single largest order GE had ever received. It was a savvy move by GE that kept its production levels up at a time when domestic production was at a low ebb. Ultimately, the China Ministry of Railways bought 422 C36-7s, a number nearly three times the total of all C36-7s used by railroads in North America. GE not only provided China with the locomotives but also the technology needed to rebuild them.

Although the basic equipment of the Chinese C36-7 is the same as the North American locomotives, several specifications were modified to accommodate differences

on Chinese railways. Lower maximum axle weights in China meant that the maximum base weight (subject to minor adjustments depending on modifications) of the locomotives fully loaded was just 304,235 pounds, about one-third (or 150,000 pounds) less than a standard American C36-7. This allowed for a maximum axle load of 50,705 pounds, a little more than 25 U.S. tons. Lower engine weight translates to lower tractive effort, but GE's formula for calculating starting tractive effort on Chinese C36-7s is based on 30 percent adhesion—as a result, GE specifications give the locomotives 91,270 pounds starting tractive effort. The locomotives use an 82:21 gear ratio for 73-mile-per-hour service, allowing for continuous tractive effort of 89,350 pounds at 13.8 miles per hour. The wheelbase is the same as North American locomotives (13 feet, 7 inches) but overall locomotive length is shorter—65 feet, 4 inches. Height is about the same, and the locomotives are nearly 7 inches wider. The Chinese C36-7s also feature a different cab profile with a significantly lower nose and larger forward windows. In addition, the radiators feature a slightly different profile. Another peculiarity of these units is the use of removable driving wheel tires, which was a standard steam locomotive practice.

A close-up of the fuel rack on a 7FDL-16 diesel engine. *Brian Solomon*

DASH 8

I n the early 1980s, General Electric advanced diesel-electric technology to the next stage of development by introducing onboard microprocessor controls on the DASH 8 line. Locomotive electrical control systems had utilized advances in technology, gradually progressing from traditional relay controls to solid-state electronic modules and finally to microprocessors. Using microprocessor control, GE refined locomotive component performance and improved fuel efficiency, reliability, and overall performance, as well as performance for specific applications. The successful introduction of microprocessor controls is considered one of the most significant technological advancements of the late twentieth century. Through the successful application of microprocessor controls, General Electric secured its position as the foremost builder of diesel-electric locomotives in North America.

Third or Fourth Generation?

Annalists of diesel locomotive development often classify the DASH 8 line as a member of the diesel-electric locomotive's third generation. By this assessment, the first generation comprised the machines that replaced steam: the cab units, switchers, and road switchers of the 1930s, 1940s, and 1950s. The second generation, then, were the high-horsepower locomotives starting in the 1960s, including EMD's first turbocharged diesels, such as the GP20 and SD24, as well as GE's Universal Line and Alco's Century Series.

CHAPTER 6

Opposite: General Electric's DASH 8 line was the company's key to becoming America's foremost locomotive manufacturer. On a July 1991 afternoon, a General Electric LMX B39-8 and a Burlington Northern B30-7AB lead a westbound Burlington Northern intermodal train on the Montana Rail Link east of Sand Point, Idaho. Montana Rail Link operates former Northern Pacific lines in Montana and Idaho, and handles through traffic for Burlington Northern. *Brian Solomon*

Writers such as John Kirkland, author of *The Diesel Builders* series, however, offer a different generation breakdown. In this line of thought, the diesel-electric's first generation comprised the early and experimental machines of the prewar period, while the second generation were the mass-produced postwar diesels. The introduction of AC-DC transmission in the mid-1960s is considered the third generation of development, and the DASH 8 microprocessor locomotives are deemed the fourth generation.

While these categories can help us understand the various stages of diesel development, they do not necessarily form rigid locomotive groups. Diesel manufacturers, after all, do not set out to design a "new generation," but rather look for ways to advance technology to produce more reliable and better-performing locomotives. If one manufacturer introduces an innovative cost-saving technology, other major builders are quick to follow. In microprocessor control, GE led the way, introducing its DASH 8 line a couple years ahead of EMD.

In the autumn of 1984, General Electric provided Conrail with 10 C32-8 pre-production locomotives for road testing and evaluation. These locomotives, numbered 6610 to 6619, were based in Selkirk, New York, and were largely assigned to trains using the old Boston & Albany mainline. On May 24, 1987, three C32-8s lead the eastbound SENH (Selkirk, New York–to–New Haven, Connecticut) near Washington Summit at Hinsdale, Massachusetts. Also in consist are two GE B23-7s and an EMD SW1500 destined for New Haven local service. *Brian Solomon*

Testbeds and Classics

According Greg J. McDonnell in his November 1988 *TRAINS Magazine* article, "General Electric: A Prophecy Fulfilled," GE began work on what became its DASH 8 line in 1980 and built its first experimental DASH 8 in the fall of 1982. This 3,600-horsepower machine carried the number 606 and, like earlier GE road diesels, used a 16-cylinder 7FDL diesel engine and a variation of GE 752 traction motors. However, it featured an entirely new control system and a host of new components and newly designed auxiliary systems. A second experimental machine was built in 1983, a six-motor locomotive rated at 3,900 horsepower. Following more than a year of testing, GE moved to the next stage of DASH 8 development by building four small fleets of prototypes for extensive in-service road testing on North American railroads. Each of the four fleets comprised different locomotive configurations, and all were painted in their host railroads' respective liveries.

Locomotive testing is an important element of the design process. While GE typically tests new locomotives for many hours on its East Erie Commercial Railroad, this does not necessarily replicate the circumstances that locomotives will be subjected to in actual service. History has many examples of locomotives that performed well in laboratory tests, yet failed in day-to-day service. Extensive road testing by the railroads also gave GE an opportunity to learn which features railroaders liked and disliked before incorporating them into production designs.

By taking this somewhat unusual approach, General Electric collected valuable data on real-life locomotive performance in a variety of different applications while allowing prospective customers to experiment with the locomotives without obligation to buy them. (After the test period, several railroads opted to purchase the prototypes.)

Burlington Northern received three B32-8s numbered 5497 to 5499. Each of these four-axle/four-motor (B-B wheel arrangement) units was powered by a 12-cylinder 7FDL diesel. They were rated at 3,150 horsepower, weighed 280,000 pounds fully loaded, and delivered 70,000 pounds starting tractive effort (based on 25 percent adhesion). Santa Fe received three similar B-B locomotives that were powered by 16-cylinder 7FDL engines and rated 3,900 horsepower. They carried Santa Fe numbers 7400 to 7402. Conrail had the largest test fleet, consisting of 10

Santa Fe tested three of GE's pre-production DASH 8s, model B39-8. These, like other early DASH models, were known at GE as "Classics" to distinguish them from later "Enhanced" models. Classics featured a lower-profile curved cab that gave them a humpback appearance. In January 1991, Santa Fe 7402 basks in the winter sun near Ash Hill in California's Mojave Desert. *Brian Solomon*

In 1984, Norfolk Southern tested a pair of GE C39-8 pre-production prototypes numbered 8550 and 8551. Impressed with this model, the railroad ordered the first fleet of DASH 8s. Norfolk Southern's preferred operating practice was long hood forward, and in their early years the railroad's Classic DASH 8s were normally operated nose to nose, radiator first. On Halloween morning 1987, a pair of C39-8s catches the sun while descending Attica Hill westbound on Conrail's Southern Tier Line near Dixons, New York. *Brian Solomon*

six-axle/six-motor (C-C wheel arrangement) C32-8s. These locomotives shared common characteristics with the 50 C30-7As that were built for Conrail at about the same time. They were powered by 12-cylinder 7FDLs rated at 3,150 horsepower, and fully loaded weighed 420,000 pounds and delivered 105,000 pounds starting tractive effort (based on 25 percent adhesion). Norfolk Southern received the most powerful test locomotives, a pair of C39-8s that used the 16-cylinder engine to produce 3,900 horsepower. Their weight and starting tractive effort was the same as that of the C32-8.

Conrail's C32-8s were delivered in autumn 1984 and carried the numbers 6610 to 6619. Both the C32-8s and C30-7As were based at Conrail's Selkirk Yard, located south of Albany, New York, and in their early years were largely assigned to trains on the heavily graded former Boston & Albany mainline. The B&A route is a tortuous line that traverses the rolling Berkshire Hills and has had a long history of serving as a testbed for new locomotive designs.

On May 4, 1989, Norfolk Southern C39-8 No. 8574, running long hood forward, leads an eastbound freight on the former Nickel Plate Road mainline at Lackawanna, New York. In the distance, a pair of South Buffalo Alco-GE switchers leads a local freight across a bridge over the NS train. Although long-hood operation was initially preferred, in later years, NS C39-8s were arranged to run short hood forward. *Brian Solomon*

(This is the same grade where New York Central and Lima tested the legendary 2-8-4 steam locomotive type in 1924, the first of Lima's so-called "superpower" locomotives and a type later christened the "Berkshire.") It was a perfect place for GE and Conrail to test the merits of the DASH 8 in daily heavy service. Initially the C32-8s worked in matched sets of three, producing 9,450 horsepower, enough to lift most freights over the Berkshires. Conrail eventually acquired the locomotives and throughout the 1980s and early 1990s, the 10 C32-8s were commonly used on the B&A, although they often wandered and could be found just about anywhere on the Conrail system. At times, like the other DASH 8 test fleets, they were used off-line for demonstration purposes. Conrail retained the locomotives until the railroad was broken up by Norfolk Southern and CSX in 1999, after which the unusual locomotives were finally retired. Their curved cab-roof lines and boxy hump located immediately behind the cab gave the early pre-production DASH 8s a distinctive appearance. At General Electric they were known as "Classics."

Although the 12-cylinder B32-8 and C32-8 did not attract production orders, General Electric built several fleets of pre-production DASH 8s based on the B39-8 and C39-8 designs at Erie in the mid-1980s alongside late-era Dash-7 locomotives. Conrail received a fleet of 22 C39-8s, built in summer 1986, numbered 6000 through 6021, while Norfolk Southern amassed a fleet of 139 C39-8s that included their two test locomotives. Norfolk Southern C39-8s were routinely operated long hood forward, as was contemporary NS practice. NS has since become one of GE's largest customers, and its "Classic" DASH 8s were some of the longest lived of the type. As of this writing in late 2002, there were still some Classics in service on the railroad. By contrast, the BN and Santa Fe test fleets were out of service by the early 1990s.

DASH 8 Technology

A 1984 General Electric DASH 8 promotional brochure boasted, "It's All Here, Reliability . . . Performance . . . Fuel Economy." GE explained that its design objective was to substantially reduce locomotive failures and produce a 30 percent increase in reliability. Performance was enhanced through the introduction of a better 752 traction motor and more advanced excitation control and wheel-slip control

In 1987, Union Pacific started ordering DASH 8s from GE, and eventually assembled a large fleet of DASH 8-40Cs. In November 1989, UP DASH 8-40C No. 9305, built in January of that year, leads a westbound through California's Feather River Canyon on the former Western Pacific mainline.
Brian Solomon

On September 26, 1993, a matched set of three Union Pacific DASH 8-40Cs leads the SLPA-Z, a priority intermodal train, westbound in the Feather River Canyon at Pulga, California. *Brian Solomon*

Below: General Electric builder's plate on a brand-new Conrail DASH 8-40C. *Brian Solomon*

systems, while computer-activated auxiliaries would lower the draw on the engine to reduce fuel consumption.

In the DASH 8 designs, General Electric employed the latest and most refined versions of its primary components: the FDL diesel engine and 752 traction motors. Decades of continuous development and improvements from road service experience had made these the foundation for GE's success. The FDL engine had powered GE locomotives for more than a quarter-century, while the modern 752 nose-suspended motor was the fruit of roughly a century of continuous research and development. In its literature, General Electric highlighted the motor's design qualities and noteworthy performance characteristics, including a broad speed range, low continuous operating speed, and the ability to deliver high tractive effort. It is a simple motor to maintain, with easy-to-inspect brushes and sealed armature bearings that do not require regular lubrication. With its modern motors, GE advertised that it had reduced operating temperatures significantly while providing greater resistance to moisture. By employing a specialized

Conrail DASH 8-40Bs Nos. 5060, 5061, and 5062 were only a few days old when they were photographed on the former New York Central Water Level Route at Wayneport, New York, at 4:53 P.M. on May 4, 1988. Conrail 5060 is the class leader of an order for 30 DASH-40Bs built for Conrail in spring 1988. *Brian Solomon*

epoxy varnish insulation, GE motors also offered superior heat transfer, while experiencing minimal moisture absorption without suffering from unwanted grounding. GE explained that its traction motors employed a Teflon "creepage band" and "motor frame flash ring" combined with glass banding on the commutator end of the armature to limit potential damage from motor flashover. This is a serious electrical short that can occur in traction motors at higher speeds when current fails to follow the normal desired path. The 752AG motor introduced with the DASH 8 exhibited further improvements that enabled GE to boost continuous tractive effort ratings by 5 to 11 percent on the DASH 8 locomotives over early models.

Among the other significant advances of the DASH 8 line was the development of a sufficiently powerful traction alternator/rectifier that is capable of supplying high voltage and high current to motors without the need for transition switching. In earlier locomotive designs the alternator could not supply both sufficient current for starting and the voltage needed for high speeds. To overcome this inadequacy,

an electrical transmission was needed to match output characteristics of the alternator (or generator in pre–AC-DC rectifier locomotives, such as the U25B) with the needs of the motors. This transmission serves a function similar to that of a mechanical gearbox in an automobile, although electrical steps are used instead of mechanical gears. As the speed of the locomotive increases, so does the need for voltage. To accommodate the need for greater voltage, motors are reconfigured—a process known as *transition*—through various arrangements of series and parallel connections. In early diesels, such as the Alco-GE RS-2, the locomotive engineer manually initiated the transition; in later locomotives, transition functions were automated. In most GE locomotives, transition takes place in the motor connections, although in some late-era Dash-7s, transition functions are accomplished by a switch-gear in the traction alternator.

Because the need for transition was a compromise, the system had several drawbacks. As is the case of shifting gears using a clutch in a manual automotive gearbox, there is a momentary power drop during transition. Different locomotives

119

working together in a consist enter transition independently based upon each machine's design characteristics. While similar locomotives should enter transition in harmony with one another, dissimilar locomotives may have different transition characteristics and enter transition at different times. While this doesn't necessarily result in lower efficiency, it can produce a rough ride. In the most extreme circumstances, as when a heavy train ascends a steep grade, rough transitions can result in broken knuckle couplers when locomotives and cars slam together. Overcoming the need for transition in DASH 8 locomotives allowed GE to wire the locomotives in full parallel, providing superior adhesion characteristics—locomotives no longer needed to drop load while performing transition functions. Also, since the complex electrical switch-gear required to make transition was eliminated, the DASH 8 was a simpler machine electrically.

Microprocessor control was the key to the DASH 8 design. Although computers had been around for many years, it wasn't until the early 1980s that technological advances made possible powerful computers that were both

Above: Union Pacific DASH 8-40Cs Nos. 9180 and 9292 run "elephant style" (nose to tail) and catch the glint of the evening sun at Reno Junction, California, in November 1989. Union Pacific assigned its fleet of high-tech GEs to road service on its transcontinental routes, making them a common sight along the old Western Pacific, a railroad that UP had absorbed at the end of 1981. *Brian Solomon*

Right: On the morning of April 28, 1989, a matched set of three Conrail DASH 8-40Bs leads double-stack container train TV-200 eastward along the Delaware River near Hancock, New York. Conrail 5073 features a recently applied nose banner, featuring a stylized image of shaking hands and promoting better labor-management relations. *Brian Solomon*

small enough and sufficiently rugged to fit on a locomotive and endure the harsh conditions imposed by a railroad environment. Only a few years prior to the development of the first DASH 8 prototypes, serious computers had been large machines that filled entire rooms and required constant attention and careful climatic control in order to perform properly. The initial DASH 8 models employed three different computers that were situated in the locomotive's electrical cabinet. Each computer had its own specialized functions and managed specific locomotive systems to achieve optimum performance. Computer controls constantly compared input data collected from a multitude of sensors, analyzed the data, and accordingly regulated individual system performance through electrical adjustments. One computer oversaw overall locomotive performance, another strictly managed the excitation of the main alternator, and the third regulated the auxiliary systems.

On the DASH 8, the computers are designed to prevent component damage by de-rating or shutting down systems before perceived flaws get out of control. For example, computers sense symptoms that precede traction motor flashover and introduce corrective action before flashover can occur, minimizing the instances of this destructive event.

Another advantage of DASH 8 computer control is a detailed set of diagnostic tools that gives operators and mechanics the ability to diagnose and keep track of flaws. Diagnostics also provide a detailed record of a locomotive's performance history, making preventative maintenance easier and allowing mechanics to overcome problems before they become serious. It also helps GE track reoccurring problems in the event of flawed components or other system inadequacies.

On DASH 8 locomotives, computer diagnostic panels are located on the rear cab wall. The interactive diagnostic

In June 1988, New York, Susquehanna & Western took delivery of four DASH 8-40Bs for intermodal service. This was an unusual order for a regional railroad, since by the 1980s few smaller lines were acquiring new locomotives. In April 1989, NYS&W No. 4002 leads DHT-4C, a Sealand double-stack container train, past an antique Union Switch & Signal semaphore on the former Erie Railroad mainline near Cameron Mills, New York, in the Canisteo River Valley. Technically, this was a Delaware & Hudson train running on trackage rights over Conrail. *Brian Solomon*

Overpressure"; and "SHUTDOWN: Electrical Control Problem." Less serious messages include: "Load Limited: Low Oil Pressure"; "Load Limited: Traction Motors Cut Out"; and "May Reduce Load: Radiator Fan Problem."

On DASH 8 locomotives, GE also introduced an entirely new method to drive auxiliary equipment such as the electrical equipment blowers, air compressor, radiator fan, and dynamic brake fans. On Universal Line and Dash-7 locomotives these auxiliaries were mechanically driven from a large shaft off the FDL engine. (As mentioned in the previous chapter, later Dash-7 models employed an eddy-current clutch on the radiator fan that was only operated when needed.) The disadvantage with this arrangement is that auxiliaries operate continuously regardless of whether they are needed or not, causing a drain on the engine and wasting fuel. It also results in unnecessary wear to auxiliary systems that reduces reliability and increases maintenance. With the DASH 8, the 7FDL diesel engine drives an auxiliary alternator that produces three-phase AC current to provide power for auxiliary systems that are powered by three-phase motors. (The auxiliary alternator also provides power for charging batteries and alternator excitation.) The AC motors are maintenance-free, as they do not require brush changes and are carefully regulated by computer and only switched on when conditions require. For example, pre–DASH 8 locomotives used a single mechanically driven equipment blower that ran continuously at a rate governed by engine speed. On the DASH 8, three separate blowers are employed: one for the alternators, rectifier diodes, and excitation regulators, and two to cool traction motors and related equipment with one blower for each truck.

Symphony of Sounds

A DASH 8's automated auxiliary controls result in the locomotive producing a variety of sounds at different times. The sounds produced are a peculiarity of GE's modern technology, but they seem more prevalent because the mufflers used on DASH 8s keep traditional engine noises at a minimum. If you listen to a DASH 8, or other modern GE idling, you will note several distinct sounds that reveal what is going on inside the locomotive.

The constant *ticka ticka ticka* is the noise made by engine valve gear at low cylinder pressure. The valves continue to make noise when the locomotive is throttled up,

In spring 1989, backed by CSX, the New York, Susquehanna & Western placed a second order for GE DASH 8-40Bs. These locomotives were needed while NYS&W was the designated operator of the bankrupt Delaware & Hudson. Seen on April 28, 1989, NYS&W 4020 was fresh out of GE's Erie Plant when it was photographed in the morning sun at "BD" in Binghamton, New York, after running overnight from Buffalo. *Brian Solomon*

readout, known in GE terminology as a Diagnostic Display Panel and abbreviated DID, replaces a multitude of conventional warning lights used on earlier locomotives. In situations where a serious system flaw or component failure occurs (what GE terms a *fault*), the computer sounds an audible alarm to warn the locomotive engineer. Unlike on earlier locomotives, on which an alarm could indicate a variety of problems that the crew would then have to troubleshoot, on DASH 8 locomotives the alarm bell is typically accompanied by a description of the problem. GE lists potential faults in order of severity. Among the most serious alarm messages are: "WARNING! Air Compressor Does Not Pump"; "SHUT-DOWN: Low Oil Pressure"; "SHUTDOWN: Crankcase

but these sounds are usually drowned out by exhaust roar. Periodically, the locomotive will produce a distinctive space-age *Vhoooop!* This is the big radiator-fan motor starting, indicating that the engine requires cooling. A *pfft pfft pfft* spitting sound is made by water purge valves expelling water from the air reservoir. This tends to be more prevalent on damp days. Lastly, GE's motor-driven air compressor kicks in from time to time when air pressure drops below an established threshold. When this happens, the locomotive issues a sudden *Budda gidda gidda . . .Pffscht!*

DASH 8 Production

GE used a modular approach in the construction of its DASH 8 locomotives. Although several different models were offered, they were basically different configurations of established modules. According to Greg McDonnell in "General Electric: A Prophecy Fulfilled," from the November 1988 issue of *TRAINS Magazine*, this approach eased construction, reduced building time, and improved component testing. In 1987 and 1988, GE built two fleets of four-motor, high-horsepower locomotives that carried the B39-8 designation. These locomotives were more advanced than the early pre-production units and incorporated several external changes such as boxy, squared-off cabs, and angled radiator vents. GE distinguished these locomotives from the "Classics" by calling them "Enhanced" DASH 8s. *The Contemporary Diesel Spotter's Guide* designates these locomotives B39-8Es to reflect the differences between the Enhanced production units and Classic B39-8 prototypes painted for Santa Fe. GE built 40 of these locomotives for Southern Pacific (which designated them B39-8), and 100 for General Electric's LMX subsidiary for use as a lease fleet. These latter locomotives were painted gray, white, and red (similar to some other GE demonstrators) and lettered for GE and LMX, and were leased to Burlington Northern on a "power by the hour" basis. With this arrangement, the railroad only pays for the work done rather than the whole locomotive. The LMX fleet was the first full-service maintenance contract won by General Electric. The maintenance facility was located at the former Burlington shop in Lincoln, Nebraska. This set an important precedent. Today, GE maintains most of its modern GE fleets at shops all across North America.

Southern Pacific B39-8s (SP class GF439) make a rare appearance on Donner Pass on June 7, 1992. Against a stormy sky, SP No. 8007 leads the second RORV-M (Roper Yard, Utah, to Roseville, California). This 4,433-ton train is descending the Sierra Nevadas on the original 1860s alignment at Yuba Pass, California. Four-motor GEs were more commonly assigned to the Sunset Route. *Brian Solomon*

B39-8 and C39-8 models, respectively. Despite this official change, many railroads continued to list GE locomotives by the older designation system, thus referring to a DASH 8-40C as C40-8. During the first few full years of DASH 8 production, beginning in 1987, the majority of locomotives were either four- or six-motor 4,000-horsepower models. With these two basic types, GE claimed and held the title as America's most prolific domestic locomotive manufacturer.

The DASH 8-40C was initially the most popular model and *The Contemporary Diesel Spotter's Guide* indicates that 581 were sold domestically. The locomotives featured the boxy conventional cab profile exhibiting the "meaner," more linear appearance of the production DASH 8 line. According to GE data, it shared the same external dimensions with the C39-8 and exhibited most common performance characteristics, while producing slightly higher horsepower.

At the end of 1987, Union Pacific, which had neither experimented with nor ordered any of the early DASH 8 models (instead acquiring hybrid C36-7s through Missouri Pacific), ordered the first and largest fleet of DASH 8-40Cs. As is often the case with new diesel acquisitions, Union Pacific traded in worn-out locomotives for the latest model; in this case UP sent GE its well-used U30Cs. General Electric recycled some components, and the first UP DASH 8-40Cs rode on refurbished U30C trucks. Union Pacific's DASH 8-40Cs weighed just 391,000 pounds, several tons less than GE's published maximum of 420,000 pounds for the model. Ultimately, Union Pacific placed five orders for this model, consisting of more than 255 locomotives that were numbered in the 9100 to 9350 series. Union Pacific's DASH 8s were assigned to its general road pool, but in their early days were typically operated in matched sets of two to four units. In the late 1980s, they were a common sight on UP's busy Overland Route, where they could be found hauling long drags and grain trains across Nebraska and Wyoming, as well as leading intermodal trains, such as priority APL (American Presidents Line) double-stack trains to West Coast ports.

Conrail acquired a relatively small fleet of just 25 DASH 8-40Cs (which had C40-8 printed on their sides below the road number) that were delivered in spring 1989. Conrail was one of GE's best customers throughout the 1980s, and these six-motor locomotives joined the railroad's

As the DASH 8 line matured, several standard types were offered and a new designation system was developed. Taking advantage of the higher quality conveyed by its DASH 8 line, GE incorporated the "DASH" in its new designations. Concurrent with this change, General Electric also boosted the output of its 16-cylinder models to an even 4,000 horsepower. The resulting models were the DASH 8-40B and DASH 8-40C, which replaced the already GE-intensive road fleet. Initially, they tended to operate in matched pairs, but could soon be found in combination with other types and were used in a great variety of road service.

In 1989, CSX bought DASH 8-40Cs, its first DASH 8s, and the first in a long line of high-tech General Electric locomotives that have dominated that railroad's fleet ever since. Since this first DASH 8 order, CSX has been a very steady GE customer and in recent times has only sampled EMD products. As a testimony to the DASH 8 design, GE won another longtime EMD customer in 1989. Chicago & North Western—which, with the exception of seven U30Cs, had ignored General Electric road diesels—bought a fleet of DASH 840Cs based on the UP's experience with them. At first, these locomotives were assigned to C&NW's Powder River coal services. They were restricted from many C&NW routes, because their unusually heavy axle loads put them above existing limits and they lacked necessary signaling equipment for mainline service. C&NW placed successive orders for DASH 8-40Cs, and in later years operational limitations were overcome, allowing the locomotives to be used in a variety of mainline services.

While the six-motor DASH 8-40C dominated orders for new locomotives, GE had considerable success selling the four-motor DASH 8-40B, as well. This model shared external characteristics with the DASH 8-40C and had common dimensions with the B39-8, which it superseded. The DASH 8-40B was nominally heavier and had slightly better traction characteristics than the B39-8. According to GE specifications, it delivered 69,200 pounds at 18.6 miles per hour. As with other high-horsepower, four-motor diesels, the DASH 8-40B was intended for fast freight. Intermodal giant Conrail was the first railroad to purchase the model. Its first DASH 8-40Bs were delivered to the railroad at Erie, Pennsylvania, at the end of April 1988 and were immediately dispatched westward on a high-priority intermodal train. Conrail's DASH 8-40Bs were numbered in the 5060 series following the B36-7s delivered a few years earlier. Conrail initially operated the DASH 8-40Bs (which it designated B40-8) in three-unit sets, providing intermodal trains with a high horsepower-per-ton ratio and thus the fast acceleration needed to maintain tight schedules. Conrail's intermodal network typically operated on passenger-train-like scheduling and was one of the most impressive high-speed

freight networks in the United States. Gradually, the DASH 840Bs were mixed with the B36-7s and EMD-built GP40-2s in intermodal service. A few months after delivery, Conrail affixed to the noses of the DASH 8-40B fleet white banners that featured a pair of stylized shaking hands and proclaimed "Labor/Management Project. Working Together for Safety Service Success."

Santa Fe and Southern Pacific, also major intermodal carriers operating significant fleets of high-horsepower GE four-motor diesels, both ordered DASH 8-40Bs, as well. Santa Fe's were among the last new locomotives painted in its blue-and-yellow scheme. These locomotives were well suited to Santa Fe's "intermodal expressway" that connected Chicago and California cities with a regular parade of fast

Chicago & North Western had been a solid EMD customer for decades, until GE developed the DASH 8 line. From that time onward, C&NW bought only GE locomotives, assembling a sizable fleet of DASH 8, DASH 9, and AC4400CWs. Initially, its DASH 8-40Cs, such as No. 8548, were limited to Wyoming coal service. In later years they were cleared for mainline work and were common on the transcontinental route to Chicago. *Brian Solomon*

The Clinchfield was a north–south railroad running through the Blue Ridge Mountains from Elkhorn City, Kentucky, to Spartanburg, South Carolina. The line was built late and at a high cost, with numerous bridges and tunnels. The Clinchfield lost its independence years ago and is one of the components of the modern-day CSX. On February 8, 2002, a pair of CSX DASH 8-40Cs leads a southbound train across the high trestle at Speers Ferry, Virginia. *T.S. Hoover*

piggyback trains. Southern Pacific's DASH 8-40Bs were adorned in its standard gray and scarlet paint, and were typically operated with its B39-8s. SP's DASH 8s were primarily Sunset Route power, where they were assigned to high-priority intermodal trains, including double-stacks operating east of Los Angeles. These locomotives were occasionally assigned to other routes but were only rarely operated on SP's Overland Route between Oakland, California, and Ogden, Utah.

The smallest fleet of DASH 8-40Bs was acquired by the Northeastern regional railroad New York, Susquehanna & Western. The NYS&W achieved some notoriety in 1945 as the first Class I carrier to complete dieselization, which it accomplished with a small fleet of Alco-GE S model

switchers and RS-1 road switchers. It was also one of the few Northeastern lines to escape inclusion in Conrail in 1976. In the early 1980s NYS&W expanded its operations by acquiring former Lackawanna lines north and west of Binghamton, New York, along with haulage rights over Conrail's former Erie Railroad Southern Tier Route to Binghamton from NYS&W's operational base in Little Ferry, New Jersey. In the mid-1980s, NYS&W became the eastern terminus for intermodal stack train traffic by teaming up with the Delaware & Hudson and CSX to offer an alternative to Conrail. Initially, NYS&W hauled double-stack trains using a fleet of secondhand Alco C430s acquired from Conrail. Later, it purchased a fleet of ex–Burlington Northern SD45s and F45s that proved more reliable and more capable of handling the railroad's growing intermodal traffic. Typically, NYS&W locomotives operated west of Binghamton to Buffalo, New York, over the former Erie mainline using Delaware & Hudson trackage rights. In the spring of 1988, NYS&W acquired four new DASH 8-40Bs built to Conrail specifications to haul its stack trains. These locomotives were evenly numbered from 4002 to 4008 in accordance with Susquehanna practice, in which the first two digits reflected horsepower output. They were painted in the railroad's attractive yellow-and-black livery, giving them a traditional appearance.

Coincidental with this acquisition was the bankruptcy of Delaware & Hudson in June 1988. D&H had been operated by Guilford since 1984, but in the summer of 1988, Susquehanna was appointed the designated operator of the D&H, which put the railroad in a need for more heavy motive power. In the short term, NYS&W leased locomotives from a variety of sources, including Norfolk Southern, which leased a small fleet of C30-7s. NYS&W, with financial assistance from CSX, ordered an additional 20 DASH 8-40Bs, and for a couple of years, NYS&W's DASH 8-40Bs were standard road power on D&H freights. Although Susquehanna was among the bidders for control of the D&H, ultimately Canadian Pacific acquired the property, at which time CSX assumed ownership of the second 20 NYS&W DASH 8-40Bs. These were quickly repainted in CSX's colors and numbered in the 5900 series after that line's B36-7s. The remaining four NYS&W GEs continued to work for their original owner.

Another fleet of four-motor DASH 8s comprised 45 DASH 8-32Bs ordered by Norfolk Southern in 1989. These locomotives were nearly 3 feet shorter and weighed about 2 tons less than the DASH 8-40Bs. They were rated at 3,200 horsepower and powered by a 12-cylinder 7FDL engine.

New Santa Fe DASH 8-40BWs lead train 197 past vintage Union Switch & Signal lower-quadrant semaphores on the Southern Pacific's Tucumcari Line at Torrance, New Mexico, on May 5, 1991. Rerouted due to a derailment on the Santa Fe's El Paso subdivision, this expedited train of auto parts and merchandise is detouring over its competitor's rails to reach El Paso. The undulating profile of this high-desert mainline will be no match for this high-horsepower trio of locomotives. *Photo by Tom Kline*

Santa Fe train 199, the line's premier Chicago–Bay Area intermodal, glides through Franklin Canyon at Christie, California, behind five DASH 8-40BWs on the afternoon of March 18, 1993. *Brian Solomon*

In January 1991, four Santa Fe safety-cab DASH 8-40BWs and one standard-cab DASH 8-40B lead a once-weekly Maersk double-stack train across the Mojave Desert near Goffs, California. Combined, these five GEs produce a total of 20,000 horsepower. Santa Fe reintroduced its famous warbonnet livery in 1989 on its Super Fleet locomotives. *Brian Solomon*

The Widecab Revolution

In recent years, American diesel-electrics have taken on a new appearance. Since 1989, nearly all railroads have adopted an improved cab style known as the *North American Safety Cab*, and frequently referred to as *widenose cabs* or *widecabs*. Though not specifically related to DASH 8 technology, GE implemented the design during the height of DASH 8 production. The root of the North American Safety Cab stems from the elimination of the caboose in the mid-1980s and other changes in labor practices, including the extension of crew districts to cover hundreds of miles. One of the most progressive railroads in implementing new crew arrangements was the Santa Fe. It offered concessions to operating personnel, including an improved working environment—specifically a better locomotive cab. In "Cab of the Future" (December 1990, *TRAINS Magazine*), Steve Schmollinger listed objectives that Santa Fe and its crews desired from a new cab design, including a safer, quieter space with more ergonomic arrangements for the locomotive engineer. Modern road locomotives had

evolved from the road-switcher type first developed in the 1940s. However, since modern operations often require long mainline runs that do not require switching, the cab and control stand arrangement that made sense for a road switcher was deemed inadequate by engineers who faced forward for hours at a time. Schmollinger noted that Santa Fe borrowed a modern Canadian National EMD SD50F for evaluation while drawing inspiration from its own cowl types in the design of the new, modern cab. Although Santa Fe considered a modern cowl-type locomotive along the lines of those used by Canadian roads, it decided against it and instead worked with both General Electric and EMD in the design of a new cab that incorporated soundproofing, desktop controls, a better forward view, and greater structural safety to protect crews in the event of a collision.

In 1988, GE outfitted its four-motor DASH 8 testbed as a safety-cab prototype. However, EMD sold the first modern safety-cab locomotives to an American line, building SD60Ms for Union Pacific in 1989. General Electric followed about a year later with its DASH 8-40CW (W to

General Electric built 20 four-axle safety-cab locomotives for Amtrak in December 1991. Although the DASH 8-32BWH was unique to Amtrak, the type shared many common attributes with Santa Fe's DASH 8-40BWs, and externally the two types are nearly identical. The Amtrak locomotive uses a 12-cylinder engine and produces 3,200 horsepower. It also has an additional alternator to generate head-end electricity for passenger cars. *Author collection, photographer unknown*

reflect the wider cab design), which also was first sold to Union Pacific. Within a few years most of GE's customers were purchasing locomotives with North American Safety Cabs, and only a few lines, such as Norfolk Southern, continued to order the traditional cab design.

Warbonnets

Soon after Union Pacific's first safety cabs, Santa Fe bought fleets of high-horsepower, four-axle locomotives from both EMD and GE. Santa Fe had recently reintroduced its colorful red, yellow, black, and silver "warbonnet" livery—a color scheme that was designed by Electro-Motive artist Leland A. Knickerbocker and which had graced its passenger locomotives from the 1930s until the end of passenger service in 1971. From 1990 until Santa Fe merged with

Burlington Northern in 1995, all of its new road locomotives were dressed in the warbonnet scheme and assigned to the railroad's premier Super Fleet, a name coined to recall the days of the railroad's best-known passenger train, the *Super Chief.*

Between 1990 and 1992, GE built a fleet of 83 DASH 8-40BWs for Santa Fe, a model unique to the railroad. Numbered in the 500 series, they were assigned to the railroad's fastest high-priority intermodal trains, including the famous QNYLA, a transcontinental run between the New York City metro area and Los Angeles and operated in conjunction with Conrail, and the 199/991 trains that connected Chicago and the California Bay Area. These trains operated on passenger-train-like schedules and were among the fastest freight trains in the world, based on end-to-end timing. In order to keep its priority trains moving, Santa Fe used a very high horsepower-to-ton ratio and ensured that the premier trains were assigned the very best locomotives. Typically, four or more DASH 8-40BWs were used on the 199/991 train. The 500 series GEs were preferred on this run, because they exhibited superior traction qualities when climbing through California's Tehachapis, an especially steep and sinuous mountain crossing. When Santa Fe's DASH 8-40BWs were new, they were among the best-performing locomotives in the United States.

Similar to Santa Fe's 500 series were 20 DASH 8-32BWHs built for Amtrak, which Amtrak interestingly also numbered in the 500 series. These locomotives share most external dimensions with the Santa Fe 500s but feature a few significant internal differences. The DASH 8-32BWH uses a 12-cylinder engine instead of a 16-cylinder and produces 3,200 horsepower for traction. An extra alternator is

Above: "Quality" was the buzzword of the 1990s, which many American railroads incorporated into their corporate vocabularies. A new Conrail DASH 8-40BW features a "Quality" variation of the Conrail livery. *Brian Solomon*

Left: The first North American Safety Cab locomotives ordered by a major eastern carrier were General Electric DASH 8-40CWs for Conrail in 1990. In September 1991, Conrail BUOI (Buffalo, New York, to Oak Island, New Jersey) sports a new DASH 8-40CW at Linden, New York, on the former Erie mainline. *Brian Solomon*

used to produce head-end power for passenger cars (thus the H at the end of the designation). Amtrak dressed the locomotives in an entirely new livery, a radical and refreshing change from the staid and well-worn "red-white-and-blue stripes on platinum mist" livery that had adorned the majority of Amtrak's F40PH locomotives since the 1970s. The scheme was compared to the coloration used by Pepsi on its 12-ounce cola cans, leading to the DASH 8-32BWH's unofficial "Pepsi Can" moniker. Some pundits have claimed this was the most attractive of all Amtrak liveries. The locomotives were initially assigned to Amtrak's West Coast services and were commonly used on the *Coast Starlight*, *San Joaquin*, and *Capitol* trains. Amtrak's order for DASH 8-32BWHs was a prelude to the development of the GENESIS type.

Super 7

By the late 1980s, trends in locomotive development had produced high-horsepower, high-tech models at a relatively high price. In order to expand its market, General Electric developed its Super 7 line of inexpensive and moderate-horsepower diesel-electrics. Initially GE intended to assemble Super 7 models using recycled components from older U-series Dash-7 locomotives. By melding traditional components with modern control systems and other technological advances, GE could offer a high-quality locomotive with greater fuel efficiency and better reliability than its older designs. Externally, Super 7s resembled contemporary DASH 8 locomotives; they featured the larger, boxy cab and DASH 8–style radiators, among other DASH 8 elements. By using DASH 8 electronics, GE estimated a 10 to 20

percent improvement in fuel efficiency over its 1970s-era Universal Line and Dash-7 locomotives. Super 7 locomotives used SENTRY wheel-slip control for improved tractive effort; and operator amenities such as a bigger and more comfortable cab, a modern toilet, and built-in refrigerator improved the working environment offered by traditional GE road locomotives. The total cost of the locomotive was kept down by using recycled 7FDL prime movers, GE 752 traction motors, trucks, and locomotive platforms, all of which are among the most expensive individual components in a new GE locomotive.

The first commercial Super 7s were built for the Pennsylvania-based Monongahela Railway in 1989, using components from retired Western Pacific U23Bs. They were built at the old Montreal Locomotive Works plant in Montreal, a facility in which many Alco-GE locomotives had been built in the late 1940s and early 1950s. Monongahela received 11 Super 7-B23s (sometimes described as B23-Super 7) rated at 2,250 horsepower. The railroad was closely involved with the development of the Super 7 and, according to the book *Monongahela* by Harry Stegmaier and Jim Mollison, the railroad's president, Paul Reistrup, suggested the Super 7 branding to GE.

General Electric offered two primary Super 7 models for the domestic market—the Super 7-B23 and Super 7-C30—and built demonstrators of both types. The external

Being tested on Southern Pacific's heavy trains in the Gulf Coast region, GE's Super 7 demonstrator No. 3001 prepares to depart Galveston, Texas, on August 24, 1996, with a molten sulfur drag. *Tom Kline*

Union Pacific was the first American line to receive locomotives with the newly introduced North American Safety Cab. EMD SD60Ms were delivered in early 1989, followed by GE's DASH 8-40CW later that year. Today, nearly all new American road freight locomotives use this cab design. A pair of Union Pacific DASH 8-40CWs works eastbound with a heavy Powder River coal train at Colo, Iowa, on the former Chicago & North Western mainline, as its aluminum hoppers reflect the rosy glow of a red October sunrise. *Brian Solomon*

dimensions of locomotives can vary depending on the recycled platforms used in the manufacture of different machines. The figures here are based on GE's published data. The Super 7-B23 is a four-axle/four-motor machine and measures 60 feet, 2 inches long; 14 feet, 11-1/2 inches tall; and 10 feet, 3 inches wide. It uses 40-inch wheels and a standard 83:20 gear ratio for 70-mile-per-hour operation. Maximum weight is 272,000 pounds, and the continuous tractive effort rating is 64,000 pounds at 10.2 miles per hour. The engine is GE's standard 12-cylinder 7FDL rated at 2,250 horsepower.

The Super 7-C30 is a six-motor machine and has nearly the same external dimensions as the C30-7, although it's slightly wider and shares styling with DASH 8 types. It uses the same size wheels and same gearing as the Super 7-B23. Based on 410,000 pounds maximum weight, a Super 7-C30 develops 96,000 pounds continuous tractive effort at 9.1 miles per hour. It uses a 16-cylinder 7FDL rated at 3,000 horsepower.

One of the largest orders for Super 7s came from Mexican railway Ferrocarriles Nacionales de México, which was so impressed with the type that it ordered a large fleet of 3,000-horsepower units using all new components rather than recycled parts. They were painted in the railroad's attractive two-tone blue and received its five-digit numbers.

Overall, the market for new-built (or remanufactured) moderate-horsepower locomotives remained comparatively soft through the 1990s. This may be attributed to the large numbers of third-party leased locomotives in the 3,000-horsepower range already available to North American railroads. These locomotives became available as the largest railroads bought large numbers of new locomotives and sold older locomotives to leasing companies, including GE subsidiaries, instead of trading them in or scrapping them, as had previously been common practice.

Amtrak's unique DASH 8-32BWHs were typically assigned to western trains. On April 21, 1994, a pair leads Amtrak's *Coast Starlight*. The train is seen on Southern Pacific's Coast Line, just past the east switch of the siding at Harlem, California, in the agriculturally rich Salinas Valley. *Brian Solomon*

General Electric's Super 7 line offered an affordable locomotive that was manufactured from recycled Dash-7 and Universal components while taking advantage of increased reliability and performance, made possible by state-of-the-art microprocessor controls developed for the DASH 8 line. Mexican railway Ferrocarriles Nacionales de México was so impressed with the Super-7 that it ordered a large fleet of S7N30Cs (3,000 horsepower) using all new components. *Author collection, photographer unknown*

DASH 9

General Electric introduced its DASH 9 line in 1993. Whereas the DASH 8 had implemented a variety of significant design changes, the DASH 9 was largely a marketing tool used to distinguish GE's latest direct current–traction locomotive line that reflected a refinement of existing design. The DASH 9 was all about making a good locomotive design even better. This is a significant distinction, but one that should not be confused with GE's AC4400CW (its first alternating current–traction diesel-electric) that was introduced shortly after the DASH 9's debut.

In most respects, DASH 9 locomotives appeared and performed much like late-era DASH 8s. It expanded on DASH 8 technology in order to provide a more capable locomotive with lower lifecycle costs. After the introduction of the DASH 8 in 1984, GE implemented a number of evolutionary improvements to its locomotive line. Some innovative improvements, such as electronic fuel injection and split cooling, were offered as options on late-era DASH 8s and became standard features with DASH 9 locomotives. With the DASH 9, General Electric introduced its new and distinctive-looking HiAd (high-adhesion) truck designed to improve traction. Another change introduced with DASH 9 was the number of traction-equipment blowers. While the DASH 8 uses three blowers (one for the alternator and related equipment, and two for the traction motors with one blower directed at each truck), the DASH 9 uses only two blowers, with one large traction blower for

Opposite: Burlington Northern Santa Fe has amassed a large fleet of DASH 9-44CWs to haul merchandise and intermodal freights. Two BNSF freights pass at Darling, Arizona, on September 27, 2002. The near train is an eastbound intermodal; the far train is a westbound merchandise freight with DASH 9s working the back as Distributed Power Units (DPUs)—today's terminology for remote-control helpers. Many railroads assign DPUs in graded territory to ease operations with long, heavy trains and eliminate the need for manned helpers. *Tim Doherty*

all traction motors. Nominal external changes include a more ergonomic step and handrail arrangement for improved crew safety and comfort.

Electronic Fuel Injection and Split Cooling

Electronic fuel injection (EFI) replaced a conventional mechanical fuel injection system. EFI allows for more precise control of the diesel engine, improving power output, reducing fuel consumption, and lowering exhaust emissions. In addition, EFI enabled GE to eliminate traditional components used by mechanical fuel injection in order to improve reliability and lower maintenance costs. Years ago, exhaust emissions were only a nominal consideration in engine design. However, in recent years, more stringent governmental regulations have made lower locomotive emissions a significant goal with new designs. In order to comply with these regulations, GE improved several elements of its engine design. Introducing radiators with the split cooling arrangement is an important part of this strategy. The term *split cooling* refers to the dual water circuits used for greater cooling of diesel engine intercoolers. Improved intercooler performance allows for lower engine air-intake temperatures, reducing harmful gas emissions. In conjunction with split cooling, GE also employed a coalescer in the crankcase ventilation system to filter oil vapors from exhaust

gases. One external characteristic that identifies GE locomotives with split cooling is slightly thicker radiator wings at the back of the locomotive. The wings house the radiator cores, which are 9 inches thick, 3 inches thicker than earlier designs.

HiAd Truck

Perhaps the most identifiable feature that distinguishes DASH 9 models from DASH 8 models is GE's HiAd truck, a bolsterless truck (a bolster is a mechanical weight-bearing surface on which the wheels pivot beneath the locomotive body) designed to both reduce weight transfer and permit easier maintenance. Reducing weight transfer improves wheel-to-rail adhesion, thus the term *high-adhesion truck* from which GE coined the name HiAd. The high-adhesion truck is identifiable by its boxy, uncluttered appearance and winged journal boxes.

High Power

Higher output was also a notable feature of the DASH 9 line. Standard 16-cylinder DASH 8 locomotives had been rated at 4,000 horsepower until the early 1990s, when GE gradually increased engine output. In 1993 and 1994, GE built DASH 8-41CW locomotives, for Union Pacific and Santa Fe, featuring 4,135-horsepower output. Externally, they appeared

Chicago & North Western, the first railroad to order DASH 9s, initially assigned the locomotives in sets of three to work Powder River coal trains. On April 2, 1995, less than a month before C&NW was officially merged with Union Pacific, three of its DASH 9-44CWs lead a loaded coal train east of Rochelle, Illinois. Following C&NW's inclusion in Union Pacific, its DASH 9s became part of the UP road pool and could be found all over the Union Pacific's vast network. *Brian Solomon*

the same as the DASH 8-40CW. DASH 9 locomotives used GE's most modern DC-traction motor, the 752AH, which GE advertises as "equipped with roller support bearings and oil-filled gear cases," features designed to improve motor reliability. This motor did not make its debut on the DASH 9, however, as many late-era DASH 8s also used it.

DASH 8 Hybrids

Among the last domestic DASH 8s were a fleet of 53 locomotives built for CSX in 1994. These locomotives are best viewed as DASH 8–DASH 9 hybrids. As with the case of the late-era C36-7s, such as those ordered by Union Pacific–Missouri Pacific, the CSX DASH 8s embody features

from two locomotive lines. Numbered in the 9000 series, they incorporate DASH 9 features: split cooling and 4,400-horsepower output. However, they do not feature other notable DASH 9 characteristics such as the HiAd truck. While some sources, including CSX, list these locomotives as DASH 9s, others, such as *The Contemporary Diesel Spotter's Guide*, list them as DASH 8s.

DASH 9 Production

The first DASH 9s are normally considered those ordered by Chicago & North Western at the end of 1993. These locomotives were designated DASH 9-44CWs and use a 7FDL-16 engine to produce 4,380 horsepower (often listed

On October 20, 1994, a CSX westbound climbs through the horseshoe curve at Mance, Pennsylvania, on the Sand Patch grade. Leading the train is one of CSX's 9000-9052 series GEs, locomotives that contain some defining features of both the DASH 8 and DASH 9 series. For this reason, these unusual machines are best viewed as hybrids. *Brian Solomon*

as 4,400 horsepower). Based on information in Sean Graham-White's article "AC Revolution," published in the January 1996 issue of *Pacific RailNews*, a DASH 9-44CW with standard options and featuring 40-inch wheels with a 83:20 gear ratio can produce 140,000 pounds maximum tractive effort and 108,600 pounds continuous tractive effort (calculated using a 27 percent factor of adhesion). In the first half of 1994, Southern Pacific and Santa Fe also bought new DASH 9s. Santa Fe's were numbered in the 600 series. Following the merger with BN in 1995, BNSF made the DASH 9 its staple locomotive for its general freight pool, ordering hundreds. BNSF's typical DASH 9 uses 42-inch wheels, weighs 415,000 pounds, and delivers 105,640 pounds tractive effort at 12.9 miles per hour. BNSF applied several different paint liveries to its DASH 9 locomotives, reflecting schemes used by its heritage railroads, including Santa Fe and the Great Northern. The most recent of these

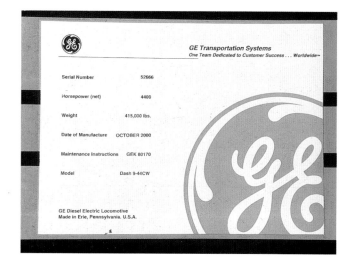

Above: Burlington Northern Santa Fe has experimented with a variety of liveries on its new locomotives. BNSF DASH 9-44CW No. 968 was the first locomotive painted in the "Heritage I" scheme shown, so named because it incorporates elements of several heritage railroad liveries. *Author collection, photographer unknown*

Right: The styles of locomotive builders' plates have evolved over the years. Compare the plate on BNSF DASH 9-44CW, built in October 2000, with the plate on a C&NW locomotive of the same model built in April 1994. *Photos by Tom Kline and Brian Solomon*

paint schemes, the so-called "Heritage II" livery, is a blend of the Santa Fe warbonnet and Great Northern schemes.

In 1994, Canadian National purchased DASH 9s with a Canadian safety cab; these are designated DASH 9-44CWL, the L indicating the four front windows of the Canadian cab. These locomotives were numbered in CN's 2500 series. While their performance characteristics are roughly the same as the BNSF models, the locomotives are slightly lighter, weighing just 390,000 pounds, and they use a slightly smaller fuel tank. BC Rail also acquired DASH 9-44CWLs. Later Canadian National DASH 9s feature widecabs with the more common two-piece windshield.

Norfolk Southern has been one of the largest users of GE DASH 9s. However, while other North American lines ordered models in the 4,400- to 6,000-horsepower range, NS specified locomotives with the more nominal output of just 4,000 horsepower. The basic building block for Norfolk Southern's modern fleet is the GE DASH 9-40CW, a DC-traction locomotive model that, as of this writing in late 2002, is only utilized by NS. In its highest throttle notch, a

Above: The engineer's desktop controls on BNSF DASH 9-44CW No. 998. The black-and-white box on top of the stand to the left is for the control of Distributed Power Units (remote-control helpers) that allow individual control of helpers using the same desktop controls used to operate the lead engines. *Tom Kline*

Left: On September 11, 2002, three BNSF DASH 9-44CWs lead an eastbound stack train along the Libby Bypass, which follows the Fisher River near Jennings, Montana. Working hard upgrade in the Flathead Mountains, these high-horsepower units maintain maximum track speed as they climb toward the Flathead Tunnel. *Tom Kline*

4,400-horsepower locomotive burns more fuel than a 4,000-horsepower model. NS does not want to pay for greater locomotive performance than it needs to move its trains, and sees a 4,400-horsepower locomotive as an unnecessary use of resources. Considering that NS operates hundreds of locomotives, even nominally lower fuel consumption adds up to considerable savings.

Norfolk Southern was also the only railroad to order DASH 9s with conventional cabs, designated DASH 9-40Cs. NS adopted the North American Safety Cab as a result of changes in locomotive-building cost structure. When the safety cab was introduced, it was offered as an option, and locomotives that used it cost more than comparable machines with conventional cabs. By the mid-1990s the situation was reversed—because most railroads were buying new locomotives with safety cabs, it became standard and the conventional cab became a specialty option. Unlike most safety-cab locomotives, Norfolk Southern DASH 9-40CWs feature conventional control stands, rather than electronic desktop controls. Desktop controls make reverse running awkward, and NS often requires road locomotives to make switching moves, so it is advantageous for locomotive engineers to be able to run comfortably in both directions.

Mechanically, Norfolk Southern's DASH 9-40CWs are basically the same as standard DASH 9-44CWs. The primary difference is in the locomotive's engine governing unit (EGU), the onboard computer that runs the diesel engine. By using a different software strategy, Norfolk Southern DASH 9 EGUs limit maximum output in "Run-8" (the highest throttle position). There is no appreciable difference in output in the lower throttle positions. Furthermore, a key-operated switch behind the engineer can be used to revert the EGU software strategy to that of standard 4,400-horsepower maximum output. Norfolk Southern's conventional-cab DASH 9-40Cs are designed for a maximum weight of 410,000 pounds, but in actual service normally weigh slightly less.

Spotting DASH 9s in Action

General Electric introduced its AC4400CW just a year after the first DASH 9, and the two model lines have been built concurrently for more than eight years. Several railroads have preferred direct current locomotives, while others prefer ACs. The many external similarities between the DASH 9 and AC4400CW lines may be confusing to the casual observer. In most respects, these machines, despite their

significantly different traction systems, share the same external appearance. One of the best spotting features, which clearly distinguishes the DASH 9 and AC4400CW, is the larger box behind the cab on the fireman's side (right-hand side when viewed head on) of the AC4400CW that contains the AC inverters. The DASH 9s do not use inverters, as the equipment is a part of AC locomotive technology.

Above: Norfolk Southern has a large fleet of DASH 9-40Cs and DASH 9-40CWs, which it uses in all types of road service. Here, a pair of DASH 9-40CWs leads a loaded coal train on the old Norfolk & Western at Bluefield, West Virginia, on October 16, 1999. *T.S. Hoover*

Right: Three Norfolk Southern DASH 9-40CWs working at full throttle lead an eastbound loaded coal train on the former Pennsylvania Railroad mainline at Lilly, Pennsylvania, in May 2002. At the rear of the train is a set of former Conrail SD40-2s. *Brian Solomon*

143

AC TRACTION

I n the early 1990s, to meet the demands of the market, both General Electric and General Motor's Electro-Motive Division independently developed modern diesel freight locomotives with three-phase alternating current traction. This advancement in North American locomotive technology required an intensive investment of time, skills, and resources, and required a substantial advance commitment to the purchase of AC locomotives on the part of American railroads. In this respect, the development of AC traction is different than most other stages of American locomotive development. As explained in previous chapters, the typical pattern of development follows the "feast or famine" purchasing cycles that have characterized locomotive acquisition since the steam era.

Technological advancement has been largely financed by individual locomotive builders during periods of slow locomotive sales in order to obtain greater market potential when economic conditions improve. By contrast, AC-traction technology was developed at a time when locomotive purchases were already robust, and in effect was financed in advance by railroads guaranteeing large AC locomotive purchases.

The development of AC traction is closely tied to the movement of unit coal trains, a big business for railroads. Modern railroads haul coal using heavy unit trains that operate directly from mines to domestic powerplants for consumption or

Opposite: CSX's commitment to General Electric enabled the builder to refine three-phase alternating current technology for American heavy-haul applications. On October 18, 2002, a CSX AC4400CW leads empty coal cars westward at Keyser, West Virginia. *Brian Solomon*

to ports for export. Coal trains have special motive power requirements, because they are extremely heavy and often operate in heavily graded territory. However, coal trains are less time sensitive than other types of rail traffic, and their cargo is not perishable. Provided coal trains are handled on predictable schedules, they don't need to be expedited, and for this reason railroads can assign less horsepower per ton.

Since economical transport is key to profits in coal transport, the large coal-hauling railroads have considered various motive power solutions that would potentially lower operating expenses. One solution was electrification. Several smaller coal-hauling lines, such as the Deseret Western, have followed this path. While large common carrier railroads have variously considered electrification, they have not embraced it because of the high costs of implementation and the inflexibility of operation. Another possibility was the development of alternative locomotive

types. In the early 1980s, Burlington Northern and CSX considered the potential of a modern coal-powered locomotive. They encouraged the ACE 3000 program, which explored the redevelopment of steam locomotive technology using microprocessor controls to optimize performance. In a related program during the mid-1980s, General Electric experimented with coal-fueled diesel technology and encouraged renewed interest in turbine locomotives. By the late 1980s, however, interest in these technologies had waned, and while the job of moving coal was left to conventional diesel-electric locomotives, the desire to reduce operating costs remained.

AC Advantages

The operating characteristics of three-phase AC motors, which are well suited to slow-speed heavy service, have been known to railroads for many years. As illustrated in Chapter 1, Great Northern selected three-phase AC traction

Southern Pacific was one of the first large users of GE's AC4400CW. It acquired them primarily for its Central Corridor and used them on heavy mineral trains operating to and from Colorado and Utah, as well as for merchandise services. In August 1995, two westbounds are powered by brand-new AC4400CWs at Pando, Colorado. A mixed freight led by No. 121 holds the siding, while a loaded iron ore train led by 186 overtakes it. At this time, SP was running roughly 20 freights a day over the former Denver & Rio Grande Western's Tennessee Pass crossing. *Brian Solomon*

for its first Cascade electrification. Yet the complexity of controlling three-phase AC had limited railroad traction applications, and for the most part DC-traction motors were the standard for most modern applications.

The inherent characteristics of three-phase AC motors make them virtually free from the overheating that plagues DC motors operating at maximum load. Where DC-traction locomotives are limited by short-time motor ratings to keep them from overheating when operating at maximum load, AC locomotives can operate at maximum load at virtually any speed with minimal risk of motor damage or stalling. In addition, three-phase AC motors offer greatly improved wheel-slip control and extended-range dynamic braking, both of which aid in operating heavy trains in graded territory while reducing costs. For example, DC-traction locomotives can only use dynamic brakes to slow a train down to about 10 miles per hour without risking motor damage. However, with AC traction, dynamic braking can be used to virtually a complete stop. This improves train handling and greatly reduces brake-shoe wear.

In addition, advanced motor control and wheel-slip control has allowed for much higher adhesion with three-phase AC traction than was possible with conventional DC traction. Traditionally, tractive effort was calculated on DC locomotives using a 25 percent factor of adhesion. Through the micromanagement of wheel slip, GE's AC diesels have dry-rail adhesion factors close to 40 percent. This translates to much higher tractive effort ratings for AC locomotives than was possible with DC locomotives of the same weight, which gives AC locomotives much greater pulling power at slow speeds.

While three-phase AC motors have been used for more than 100 years, traditionally the difficulties in controlling the motors made them impractical for most railroad traction purposes. Advances in microelectronics, however, enabled engineers to overcome motor control problems, and developments in Europe and Japan in the 1980s demonstrated the capabilities of modern three-phase traction systems, both for high-speed passenger services and relatively light freight services. In the mid-1980s, GE's competitors experimented with AC traction for heavy freight locomotives in Canada and later in the United States. By the 1990s, advances with the technology convinced American railroads to commit to adapting it for heavy service.

CSX No. 1, a GE AC4400CW, leads a loaded coal drag at the 21 Bridge east of Keyser, West Virginia, on October 17, 2002. Since buying its first AC4400CWs, CSX has assembled one of the largest fleets of AC-traction diesels in the United States. *Brian Solomon*

Burlington Northern, in effect, sponsored EMD's development through the purchase of a large fleet of SD70MACs for its Powder River coal service operations. In the summer of 1993, GE built a single AC prototype and by the end of the year, CSX—one of GE's largest customers—agreed to purchase 250 AC-traction locomotives from GE. This large order, like BN's with GM, allowed GE to refine its AC-traction technology.

GE's AC Approach

General Electric and EMD had very different approaches to the way they went about developing AC technology. EMD was the first to introduce a commercial AC-traction diesel, delivering its first BN SD70MACs at the end of 1993. It had teamed with the German firm Siemens to develop an AC-traction system based on that company's past success. General Electric, meanwhile, had already pioneered modern AC-traction technology for passenger rail and transit applications, and it simply adapted its existing technology to a heavy diesel locomotive application.

Above: General Electric's AC4400CW prototype was painted for the company and used in promotional literature. *Author collection, photographer unknown*

Right: On July 20, 1995, a pair of brand-new Southern Pacific AC4400CWs leads the first section of a westbound taconite pellet train between the remote sidings of Floy and Solitude along the former Rio Grande in the Utah desert east of Green River. The second section of the train will follow with another pair of GEs in about an hour. The iron ore was transported on a dailybasis between Minnesota's Iron Range and steelworks at Geneva, Utah. *Brian Solomon*

Above: The combination of a prolonged 3 percent eastward climb at very high altitudes and heavy trains made Colorado's Tennessee Pass one of the greatest challenges in modern railroading. This Southern Pacific coal train seen climbing through the Eagle River Canyon east of Red Cliff, Colorado, has three AC4400CWs leading, followed by four more in the middle of the train and two shoving on the rear. The two sets of helpers are controlled remotely from the cab as Distributed Power Units. *Brian Solomon*

Right: A set of four SP AC4400CWs works as mid-train Distributed Power Units on an eastbound loaded coal train seen ascending Colorado's Tennessee Pass east of Pando in September 1996. *Brian Solomon*

When EMD had the first heavy-haul, AC-traction diesel-electric on the market, it encouraged General Electric to develop a more innovative design to secure a market advantage. The two primary electrical differences between General Electric's AC-traction system and EMD's are the inverters—the banks of high-tech electrical equipment that convert direct current to a form of three-phase alternating current for traction. AC-traction motor control is accomplished by modulating current frequency using sophisticated electronic thyristor controls. Advances in semiconductor technology had permitted the development of practical frequency control equipment. Where the EMD-Siemens AC control system uses two inverters, one for each truck (one inverter controls three motors), General Electric uses six inverters per locomotive. This permits individual axle control and thus enables higher tractive effort and affords greater reliability. GE's system regulates power to each axle individually. With EMD's system, in order to prevent wheel slip, power must be reduced to three axles simultaneously, resulting in a greater loss of power. GE's control system also

Above: A pair of CSX AC4400CWs leads an empty coal train off the North Mountain subdivision on the former Chesapeake & Ohio at JD Cabin, east of Clifton Forge, Virginia, on February 24, 2002. *T.S. Hoover*

Right: Southern Pacific AC4400CW No. 267 was brand-new and had yet to work in revenue service when photographed here on July 1, 1995. *Brian Solomon*

allows for greater variance in wheel diameter, which provides a maintenance advantage. Because of this, General Electric's six-inverter system offers a distinct reliability advantage over EMD. A single inverter failure on an SD70MAC (or other EMD AC) can cut locomotive output by as much as 50 percent. However, with GE's AC locomotives, a single inverter failure will result in a maximum traction loss of 12 percent. However, in most situations a single inverter failure on a GE will not result in an appreciable change in output, because the remaining inverters have sufficient capacity to compensate for the loss of power.

The second design distinction between EMD and GE inverters is the method of cooling. Where EMD uses a chemical cooling system to disperse the intense heat generated by the inverters, General Electric uses an air cooling system. The latter is less harmful to the environment and requires less maintenance, and is therefore more economical for the user.

AC4400CW

The development of GE's AC traction immediately followed its introduction of the DASH 9 DC-traction line. Like most DASH 9 locomotives, GE's initial AC offering, the AC4400CW, was rated at 4,400 horsepower. With the exception of the traction system, most components are common between the two locomotives, and in most respects they appear quite similar. (Visual differences between the two models are discussed in Chapter 7.) The AC4400CW provided General Electric a valuable product that it used to better serve its customers and expand its customer base. In addition to securing large AC4400CW orders from CSX and Union Pacific, railroads that already operated large GE fleets, GE also took its first orders for road diesels from Canadian Pacific and Kansas City Southern, both longstanding EMD customers. GE has also sold AC models to recently privatized Mexican railways and to lines in Australia.

Left: The two large Canadian railroads have different philosophies on locomotive acquisition and application. Canadian National has remained committed to traditional DC traction, while Canadian Pacific has embraced three-phase AC technology and began acquiring AC4400CWs in 1995. *Author collection, photographer unknown*

Below: Canadian Pacific's bright red AC4400CWs are a visual treat in the scenic splendor of the Canadian Rockies. A trio of GEs leads a grain train near Canmore, Alberta, on June 28, 1998. *Eric T. Hendrickson*

Since the AC4400CW made its commercial debut in 1994, GE has continuously adjusted its design to improve performance and increase reliability. One of the early advantages offered by EMD's SD70MAC was its so-called *radial truck*, which steered through curves to reduce wheel and rail wear while improving adhesion. To match this feature, GE developed its "steerable" truck and offered it as an option on new locomotives in place of the HiAd truck introduced with the DASH 9. Several railroads have adopted the steerable truck, including CSX, Kansas City Southern, and Canadian Pacific. Another change was the introduction of Sampled Axle Speed computer software in place of the older True Ground Speed Sensor (TGSS). The new system works by monitoring individual axle speed, and is a more reliable way of controlling wheel slip than the Doppler radar employed by TGSS. According to GE, the AC4400CW is 73 feet, 2 inches long and 15 feet, 4.6 inches tall, and weighs 412,000 pounds fully serviced. It uses six 5GEB13 three-phase AC-traction motors and is geared for 75 miles per hour using 42-inch wheels.

One variation of the AC4400CW is CSX's 500 series AC4400CW. These are designed to develop more tractive effort in poor rail conditions. They are unusual in CSX's GE fleet because they have an extra 10 tons of ballast to boost their tractive effort, making them more effective in slow-speed mineral service on very steep grades. However, the maximum tractive effort on dry rails is the same as normally ballasted AC4400s with the same software package, because maximum tractive effort is limited by the software. Initially, these heavy locomotives were primarily assigned to the old Baltimore & Ohio West End grades between Grafton and Keyser, West Virginia, where a combination of multiple steep summits and very heavy unit coal trains have long presented a difficult operating environment. Kansas City Southern's AC4400CWs were built with steerable trucks and feature dual language (English and Spanish) diagnostic controls.

The AC4400CW has been one of GE's most successful locomotives, with hundreds of the type operating all over North America. While introduced as coal service locomotives, many railroads now use AC4400Cs in a variety of road services.

AC6000CW

One advantage of AC traction is the ability to produce a substantially more powerful single-unit locomotive than is

Three Canadian Pacific AC4400CWs lead train No. 874, carrying metallurgical coal destined for Chicago, past a grain elevator at Ernfold, Saskatchewan, on September 11, 1998. Canadian Pacific's early AC4400CWs used the HiAd truck, later models, such as these, use GE's "steerable" truck with 44-inch wheels. *John Leopard.*

Union Pacific acquired three new AC4400CWs built in November and December 1994, numbers 9997 through 9999. It bought additional AC4400CWs in 1996, numbered in the 6700 to 6800 series. These, combined with the former Chicago & North Western and Southern Pacific units, gave UP a fleet of over 830 AC4400CWs. Union Pacific 6779 was only two months old when photographed on the former C&NW mainline at Nelson, Illinois, in July 1996. *Brian Solomon*

A pair of Kansas City Southern AC4400CWs leads train No. 92 across the Illinois River at Watts, Oklahoma, on September 26, 2000. This 112-car coal train also sports a single remote-control AC4400CW helper shoving on the rear. *Tom Kline*

possible with traditional DC-traction motors. General Electric believed it had reached the zenith of DC-traction output with the DASH 9 and needed new technology to build a 6,000-horsepower single-engine locomotive.

Interest in 6,000-horsepower locomotives stemmed in part from the cost advantages made possible through unit reduction. In the 1960s, railroads had purchased large numbers of 3,000-horsepower locomotives in order to replace older 1,500-horsepower units on a two-for-one basis. Likewise, a 6,000-horsepower locomotive would permit a similar replacement of 1960s- and 1970s-era

3,000-horsepower machines—by the mid-1990s, most American railroads had large fleets of 3,000-horsepower locomotives nearing retirement. Both manufacturers anticipated a blossoming market for 6,000-horsepower diesels, and EMD developed its SD90MAC, while GE produced its AC6000CW. In both cases, the builders needed to develop compact diesel engines capable of producing substantially higher output.

When GE expanded the Cooper-Bessemer engine in the late 1950s, it anticipated that the design would eventually need to deliver up to 4,000 horsepower, and at 4,400

horsepower the engine had reached its maximum practical output. To obtain 6,000 horsepower, GE teamed up with the German engine manufacturer Deutz MWM to build a new diesel engine. Known as the GE 7HDL, like the 7FDL it is a four-cycle design using a 45-degree V configuration operating at 1,050 rpm.

The AC6000CW uses a larger carbody featuring much larger radiators than any earlier GE locomotive. The massive wings at the rear of the locomotive house the radiators that are designed to accommodate 550 gallons of coolant.

Several railroads were interested in the AC6000CW when the locomotive was still in its design stage. Union Pacific—which has pushed for the most powerful locomotives on the planet, from the steam turbine–electrics of the 1930s to the gas turbines of the 1940s and 1950s and the double-diesels of the 1960s—placed orders for the new 6,000-horsepower locomotives with both manufacturers well in advance of production. Perpetually power-hungry, the UP did not want to wait until GE's new 7HDL was ready. In the mid-1990s, the UP ordered a number of AC6000CW "convertible" locomotives from GE, as well as upgradeable locomotives from EMD. These AC6000CW convertibles featured the larger carbody designed to accommodate the HDL, but were initially powered with a standard 4,400-horsepower 7FDL diesel engine. (Union Pacific classified these locomotives C44/60AC.) In this way, UP could satisfy its immediate power needs, while having the option of converting the GEs to more-powerful locomotives when the new engine was ready. Later, Union Pacific and CSX both took delivery of new AC6000CWs with the 7HDL engine. CSX's locomotives are 76 feet long and 15 feet, 5 inches tall, and weigh 432,000 pounds fully serviced. Based on an article in *Diesel Era* (Volume 9, Number 6) titled "Shoving with 12,000 Horsepower" by Jay Potter, CSX's AC6000CWs were rated at 166,000 pounds continuous tractive effort using a factor of adhesion of 39.5 percent.

The AC6000CW is intended for high-priority, intermodal-type services in which railroads can make use of high

output. Initially, CSX experimented with its AC6000CWs in coal service, using them on both the head end and as helpers. Since the year 2000, many of CSX's AC6000CWs were assigned to service on former Conrail lines radiating from out of Selkirk, New York. They are commonly assigned in pairs to Water Level Route trains and those operating on Boston Line (former Boston & Albany) trains. On the latter route, pairs of the big GEs displaced EMD SD80MACs (5,000-horsepower AC units) and GE C30-7As, which had been assigned there by Conrail.

Working at 1,050 rpm, the four-cycle HDL engine sounds similar to FDL-powered GEs, although the character of the HDL sound is deeper and carries farther than that of the smaller engine.

Neither GE's nor EMD's big 6,000-horsepower locomotives have enjoyed the success of the lower-powered AC-traction diesels. For several reasons, the builders' anticipation of large-scale unit reduction schemes has not come to fruition. One has been the overwhelming success of modern 4,000- and 4,400-horsepower locomotives, machines

CSX AC6000CW rolls through CP 83 at Palmer, Massachusetts, in May 2002. These big locomotives feature GE's new 7HDL engine. *Brian Solomon*

that have demonstrated excellent reliability, dependability, and versatility. Also, a 4,000- to 4,400-horsepower unit gives a railroad greater flexibility in assigning power to a train, while a pair of 6,000-horsepower units is often either too much or too little power. In the interests of timeliness and efficiency, railroads, of course, prefer to match the power requirements as closely as possible to a train's operating needs. Assigning a train too much power is a waste of re-sources, but giving it too little power may cause it to stall or struggle over the line at reduced speed. Another issue is the reliability of 6,000-horsepower locomotives. Since fewer locomotives are assigned to a train, if a locomotive fails en route, the train has to make do with substantially less power. If, for example, CSX sends three 4,000-horsepower locomotives up a grade and one fails, the train still has 8,000 horsepower with which to make it over the road; but using just a pair of 6,000-horsepower units, a failure leaves 6,000 horsepower, just half the assigned power. And, the high cost of new diesels precludes overpowering trains to

cover for potential failures. As a result, 6,000-horsepower locomotives must have higher reliability expectations than lower-power models. While GE's AC6000CWs work daily in demanding services, hauling heavy trains up the Boston Line's Berkshire grades, their reliability has not always met expectations. As of this writing in late 2002, it seems that in the short term, railroads will prefer to acquire locomotives with lower output, and the anticipated economy offered by unit reduction will have to be met by other means.

In December 2002, General Electric announced the introduction of its new "Evolution Series" locomotive line, which incorporates a new engine design. Although specifics of the new engine have not yet been released, the intended design will generate 4,400 horsepower while complying with more stringent air-quality regulations to be imposed in 2005. GE said the new engine would use a 12-cylinder air-cooled design to reduce the production of pol-luting gases and particulates by 40 percent, while improving fuel consumption.

GENESIS

Some of the most unusual modern American diesel-electrics are General Electric's GENESIS types. In the early 1990s, Amtrak sought to replace its fleet of aging 1970s-era diesels, primarily Electro-Motive F40PHs and, to a lesser extent, GE P30CHs. Unwilling to settle for an adaptation of an existing freight locomotive for passenger work as it had with past orders, Amtrak desired a modern, lightweight state-of-the-art locomotive. Both GE and EMD entered the race to design the new type. Amtrak's specification designated the new machine AMD-103, which according to *TRAINS Magazine*, stands for Amtrak Diesel, 103 miles per hour maximum speed. General Electric was awarded the contract, and GE and Amtrak worked together in the design of a completely new diesel-electric that incorporated several European concepts. A name was needed for the AMD-103 specification, and GE held an employee contest that produced the GENESIS branding. Today, three different models fall under the GENESIS line.

The GENESIS is unique in the annals of modern locomotives. Unlike other modern American locomotives, it was specifically designed for North American passenger services and, thus is fundamentally different from modern freight locomotives. Among notable differences is the use of an integral monocoque body shell and fabricated trucks instead of a bottom supporting locomotive platform and cast trucks. Both of these designs incorporate technology derived from modern

Opposite: Unlike passenger service locomotive designs of the 1960s and 1970s, which were essentially freight locomotives adapted to passenger service, General Electric's GENESIS was a totally new locomotive, specifically designed for passenger operations. Metro-North P32AC-DM No. 205 is seen here north of Breakneck Ridge, as it races toward Poughkeepsie with a commuter train from New York's Grand Central Terminal. *Brian Solomon*

European practice, rather than traditional North American design. According to an article by Bob Johnston in the September 1993 *TRAINS Magazine*, GENESIS is the first modern North American locomotive to use fabricated trucks in place of conventional cast-steel trucks. This lightweight, high-tractive-effort, bolsterless design looks significantly different from other locomotive trucks.

Amtrak desired a powerful and fuel-efficient machine that was significantly lighter and more compact than anything else available on the market. To meet these requirements, General Electric worked with Krupp—the German firm responsible for DB AG's (German State Railway) high-speed ICE-1 body design—in the construction of a monocoque body to support the locomotive. Derived from the French, the term *monocoque* indicates the body shell is integral to the locomotive structure. In this respect, GENESIS is like the full carbody locomotives built in the 1930s, 1940s, and 1950s, such as Alco-GE's FA/FB and PA/PB models described in Chapter 2. To comply with the most restrictive mainline clearances, the GENESIS is lower and narrower than most North American road locomotives. According to GE specifications, the GENESIS Series 1 is 14 feet, 6 inches tall and 10 feet wide, making it a foot shorter and more than 2 inches narrower than a typical heavy freight diesel. As a result, GENESIS locomotives can operate on virtually all North American mainlines.

Perhaps the most striking quality of GE's GENESIS line is its radical and unorthodox appearance—it just doesn't look like anything else on American rails, past or present. According to articles by Bob Johnston in *TRAINS Magazine* and by David C. Warner in the June 1993 *Passenger Train Journal*, the GENESIS appearance was designed to fulfill

Where EMD's F40PH-2 characterized Amtrak operations in the 1970s and 1980s, GE's GENESIS is the face of the modern Amtrak. On March 25, 1995, a pair of DASH-40BWHs, otherwise known as GENESIS Series I, leads Amtrak's eastbound *Southwest Chief* toward Chicago. These first GENESIS locomotives featured fading stripes at the back of the locomotive; later GENESIS models used a solid stripe all the way back. *Brian Solomon*

Inset: This detailed view shows how the fading stripe at the back of Amtrak's GENESIS Series I locomotives was accomplished with a pattern of printer-like dots. *Brian Solomon*

Amtrak's specific desire for a modern-looking locomotive that was strong enough to withstand repeated grade-crossing collisions, yet economical to build and repair. Amtrak's designer, Cesar Vergara, avoided complex curves and used angular construction with flat surfaces. Vergara, who has enjoyed a prolific career in railroad industrial design, also developed the original GENESIS paint livery, which featured an unusual fading stripe toward the back of the locomotive. This scheme was intended to visually distinguish the locomotive from the cars, but its effect is often lost on observers, as GENESIS locomotives are often operated in multiple. Only the GENESIS Series 1 was treated with the fading stripe; later models feature solid stripes.

Unlike locomotive performance that can be quantified relatively clearly, locomotive aesthetics are purely subjective. In its early years, the GENESIS design shocked many railroad observers and generated much criticism as a result of its forward-looking and nonconventional appearance. In an August 1994 poll, the readers of *Passenger Train Journal* voted GENESIS the "Ugliest-Ever Passenger Diesel." This opinion, however, was not universally held—in the same poll, readers also listed GENESIS as the third "Most Attractive Passenger Diesel." (Electro-Motive's E8/E9 was voted first, followed by the ever-popular Alco-GE PA.) Despite dismay from some railroad enthusiasts, GENESIS has won awards for industrial design, and today Vergara is one of the most respected names in the industry.

GENESIS diesels incorporate a number of modern features, such as a cruise control speed regulation system that is similar in operation to those on modern automobiles. The cruise control only regulates engine output and does not apply braking systems. As with automotive systems, cruise control is automatically disengaged when brakes are applied. A pioneering feature of the locomotive was in the introduction of an electrically controlled "parking brake" in place of the mechanical hand brake traditionally used on most railroad equipment.

GENESIS Models

All three variations of GENESIS diesels use the same basic monocoque shell, and while they appear near identical externally, they feature significant internal differences. The Series 1, rated at 4,000 horsepower, is designated DASH 8-40BP by GE and P40 by Amtrak. The type debuted in

Three Amtrak GEs—a DASH 8-32PB sandwiched between two GENESIS Series 1s—lead the *Southwest Chief* eastbound past vintage semaphores on the Santa Fe at Chapelle, New Mexico, on September 26, 1995. The longtime domain of EMD's F40PH model, this train is now pulled by these GE units. *Tom Kline*

1993 and 44 were built at Erie between 1993 and 1994; they are numbered in the 800 series. Internally, the GENESIS Series 1 locomotives use DASH 8–era technology. The powerplant is a standard variation of GE's 7FDL-16 prime mover, and traction is provided by GE's GMG 195A1 alternator and four GE 752AH8 traction motors. A 74:29 gear ratio is used for a maximum speed of 103 miles per hour, although in actual service the Series 1 would rarely operate faster than 90 miles per hour. A 79-mile-per-hour maximum speed is typical for passenger trains on many American mainlines, unless equipped with advanced signaling systems. An auxiliary alternator, model GTA33A, drawing up to 1,072 horsepower (800 kW) provides three-phase AC for head-end power used for passenger car heating and lighting. A DASH 8-40BP weighs 268,240 pounds fully loaded and delivers 38,500 pounds continuous tractive effort at 33.3

miles per hour. Like other DASH 8 locomotives, GENESIS locomotives use integrated function electronic controls for optimal performance and reliability, and locomotive engineers run the locomotive with desktop controls. GENESIS Series 1 locomotives featured hostler's controls at the back of the locomotive to facilitate slow-speed yard moves, and as a result feature a small window on the back of the engine. Although potentially useful, this feature was dropped on the later GENESIS types.

General Electric adopted Amtrak's designation scheme for later GENESIS types. Today, the most common GENESIS is the 4,200-horsepower model P42DC, which began production in 1996. The first in the series is Amtrak No. 1, and the type now continues into the 100 series. The P42DC uses most of the same primary components employed on the DASH 8-40BP, such as the 7FDL-16 engine and conventional DC-traction motors. It incorporates DASH 9 technology

with features such as electronic fuel injection to improve locomotive performance. The P42DC is capable of 110-mile-per-hour operation, and the most recent order of the type was from Canada's VIA for 21 units in 2001. Used to replace older types in intercity services, they are VIA's first GE locomotives.

The third variety of GENESIS locomotives, and by far the most unusual, is the P32AC-DM, which is significantly different from the other GENESIS types. This specialized machine is designed for service on New York City's third-rail electrified lines—routes that once hosted New York Central's GE-built mainline electrics described in Chapter 1. It's known as a *dual-mode* locomotive (thus the DM in the designation), and is the modern-day successor to EMD's FL9, a type designed in the 1950s for the New Haven. Like the FL9, the P32AC-DM is powered by a diesel engine and can draw power from trackside direct

current third-rail using retractable third-rail shoes. Instead of the larger, more powerful, 16-cylinder 7FDL used by the other GENESIS locomotives, the P32AC-DM uses a 12-cylinder 7FDL engine that features electronic fuel injection, works at a maximum 1,050 rpm, and is rated at 3,200 horsepower. One of the P32AC-DM's most significant distinctions is that it uses three-phase alternating current traction instead of conventional DC traction. A single

Passing a boat moored in Rock Cove, Amtrak P42DC No. 196 leads the Spokane section of Amtrak's eastbound *Empire Builder* along the Colombia River at Stevenson, Washington, on July 25, 2002. The single unit will have no trouble maintaining the maximum 79-mile-per-hour speed limit with this consist on this flat water-level track. This locomotive features one of the latest Amtrak liveries, which resembles the scheme used on the *Acela Express* high-speed electric trains. *Tom Kline*

The unmistakable silhouette of a GENESIS locomotive can be seen through the trees as it races along the Hudson River in January 2000. *Brian Solomon*

Canadian passenger rail operator VIA Rail has been the most recent buyer of the GENESIS locomotive. Its contemporary livery is arguably one of the most pleasing on the GE's modern form. VIA Rail 909 is seen here at Coteau, Quebec. This photograph was made July 12, 2002, the same day as Patrick Yough's photo of the New Haven–painted P32AC-DM in New York City. *Tim Doherty*

GMG 199 alternator is used for both traction and auxiliary power. Four inverters supply controlled AC current to four GEB15 AC-traction motors. The locomotive weighs 277,000 pounds fully loaded (based on specifications from the suburban passenger carrier Metro-North) and can deliver 38,500 pounds continuous tractive effort at 33.3 miles per hour. Like the P42DC, the dual-mode P32AC-DM is designed for 110-mile-per-hour operation.

Amtrak and Metro-North both operate fleets of P32AC-DMs. Amtrak's are numbered in the 700 series and primarily used in Empire Corridor services to New York's Penn Station. Metro-North assigns its GENESIS to its routes radiating from New York's Grand Central Terminal. Four of the P32AC-DMs operated by Metro-North were purchased by the Connecticut Department of Transportation and are painted in a modern adaptation of the New Haven Railroad's famous "McGinnis" livery first used on the GE-built EP-5s. Metro-North often assigns dual-mode GENESIS locomotives to former New Haven branchline services to Danbury and Waterbury, Connecticut. The four CDOT units are used in a pool of equipment for these lines.

GENESIS and the Future

The GENESIS has been a great success. The locomotives are more powerful than older types, allowing Amtrak a unit reduction on some long-distance trains. Also, GE's microprocessor-controlled four-cycle diesel has resulted in considerable fuel savings. Since the introduction of the first GENESIS locomotive in 1993, Amtrak has gradually replaced nearly all of the older road diesels in its fleet—the once ubiquitous EMD F40PH has become a curiosity. By 2001, most Amtrak long-distance trains outside the electrified Northeast Corridor were hauled by GENESIS locomotives.

While the existing GENESIS fleet will likely represent the bulk of Amtrak's diesel fleet for some time to come, as of late 2002, the future of GE's GENESIS line was unclear. American passenger diesels represent only a small portion of the total market, and therefore it is more costly per unit to engineer substantial design changes. This is significant, because more restrictive federal emissions standards will make it impossible for American lines to purchase additional GENESIS locomotives in present configurations. Significant investment will be required to make the type compliant with future air-quality standards.

In 2001, the Connecticut Department of Transportation received four GENESIS P32AC-DMs (dual-mode diesel-electric/electrics) as part of a Metro-North order. Metro-North and CDOT operate 31 Genesis locomotives in commuter service, operating on the former New York Central and New Haven lines radiating from Grand Central Terminal. The CDOT units came delivered in an adaptation of the New Haven's 1950s-era "McGinnis" livery, commissioned by the late Joseph Snopek. Compare this locomotive with the EP-5 electrics built by General Electric in the 1950s. Train 2525 is led northbound by No. 229 at the 125th Street Station in Harlem, New York, on July 12, 2002. *Patrick Yough*

BIBLIOGRAPHY

Books

Alymer-Small, Sidney. *The Art of Railroading, Vol. VIII.* Chicago, 1908.

American Locomotive Co., General Electric Co. *Operating Manual Model RS-3.* Schnectady, N.Y., 1951.

——. *American Railroad Journal—1966.* San Marino, Calif., 1965.

Armstrong, John H. *The Railroad—What It Is, What it Does.* Omaha, Nebr., 1982.

Bruce, Alfred W. *The Steam Locomotive in America.* New York, 1952.

Burch, Edward P. *Electric Traction for Railway Trains.* New York, 1911.

Bush, Donald J. *The Streamlined Decade.* New York, 1975.

Churella, Albert J. *From Steam to Diesel.* Princeton, N.J., 1998.

Dolzall, Gary W. and Stephen F. Dolzall. *Baldwin Diesel Locomotives.* Milwaukee, Wis., 1984.

Drury, George H. *Guide to North American Steam Locomotives.* Waukesha, Wis., 1993

Farrington, S. Kip Jr.. *Railroading from the Head End.* New York, 1943.

——. *Railroads at War.* New York, 1944.

——. *Railroading from the Rear End.* New York, 1946.

Garmany, John B. *Southern Pacific Dieselization.* Edmonds, Wash., 1985.

General Electric. *New Series Diesel-Electric Locomotive, Operating Manual.* Erie, Pa., 1979.

——. *GENESIS SERIES 2 P32AC-DM Operating Manual.* Erie, Pa., 1998.

Harris, Ken. *World Electric Locomotives.* London, 1981.

Haut, F.J.G. *The History of the Electric Locomotive.* London, 1969.

——. *The Pictorial History of Electric Locomotives.* Cranbury, N.J., 1970.

Herrick, Albert, B. *Practical Electric Railway Hand Book.* New York, 1906.

Hinde, D.W., and M. Hinde. *Electric And Diesel-Electric Locomotives.* London, 1948.

Hollingsworth, Brian. *The Illustrated Encyclopedia of North American Locomotives.* N.Y., 1997.

——. *Modern Trains.* London, 1985.

Hollingsworth, Brian, and Arthur Cook. *Modern Locomotives.* London, 1983.

Keilty, Edmund. *Interurbans Without Wires.* Glendale, Calif., 1979.

Kiefer, P.W. *A Practical Evaluation of Railroad Motive Power.* New York, 1948.

Kirkland, John F. *Dawn of the Diesel Age.* Pasadena, Calif., 1994.

——. *The Diesel Builders Vols. I, II, and III.* Glendale, Calif., 1983.

Klein, Maury. *Union Pacific, Vols. I and II.* New York, 1989.

Kratville, William, and Harold E. Ranks. *Motive Power of the Union Pacific.* Omaha, Nebr., 1958.

Marre, Louis A. *Diesel Locomotives: The First 50 Years.* Waukesha, Wis., 1995.

Marre, Louis A., and Jerry A. Pinkepank. *The Contemporary Diesel Spotter's Guide.* Milwaukee, Wis., 1985.

Marre, Louis A., and Paul K. Withers. *The Contemporary Diesel Spotter's Guide, Year 2000 Edition.* Halifax, Pa., 2000.

McDonnell, Greg. *U-Boats: General Electric Diesel Locomotives,* Toronto, 1994.

Middleton, William D. *When the Steam Railroads Electrified.* Milwaukee, Wis., 1974.

——. *Grand Central . . . The World's Greatest Railway Terminal.* San Marino, Calif., 1977.

——. *From Bullets to BART.* Chicago, 1989.

——. *Manhattan Gateway: New York's Pennsylvania Station.* Waukesha, Wis., 1996.

Pinkepank, Jerry A. *The Second Diesel Spotter's Guide.* Milwaukee, Wis., 1973.

Ransome-Wallis, P. *World Railway Locomotives.* New York, 1959.

Reagan, H. C., Jr. *Locomotive Mechanism and Engineering.* New York, 1894.

Reckenzaun, Anthony. *Electric Traction on Railways and Tramways.* London, 1892.

Signor, John R. *Tehachapi.* San Marino, Calif., 1983.

——. *Donner Pass: Southern Pacific's Sierra Crossing.* San Marino, Calif., 1985.

Solomon, Brian. *Trains of the Old West.* New York, 1998.

——. *The American Diesel Locomotive.* Osceola, Wis., 2000.

——. *Super Steam Locomotives.* Osceola, Wis., 2000.

——. *The American Steam Locomotive.* Osceola, Wis., 1998.

——. *Locomotive.* Osceola, Wis., 2001.

Stevens, John R. *Pioneers of Electric Railroading.* New York, 1991.

Strack, Don. *Union Pacific 2000—Locomotive Directory.* Halifax, Pa., 2000.

Strapac, Joseph A. *Southern Pacific Motive Power Annual 1971.* Burlingame, Calif., 1971.

Books Continued

——. *Southern Pacific Review 1981*. Huntington Beach, Calif., 1982.

——. *Southern Pacific Review 1953–1985*. Huntington Beach, Calif., 1986.

Swengel, Frank M. *The American Steam Locomotive: Volume 1, Evolution.* Davenport, Iowa, 1967.

Trewman, H.F. *Electrification of Railways.* London, 1920.

Winchester, Clarence. *Railway Wonders of the World, Volumes 1* and *2.* London, 1935.

Withers, Paul K. *Norfolk Southern Locomotive Directory 2001.* Halifax, Pa. 2001

Brochures

Bearce, W.D. *Steam-Electric Locomotive.* Erie, Pa., 1939.

General Electric. *Dash 8 Locomotive Line.* (no date)

——. *GE Locomotives.* (no date)

——. *Super 7 Locomotive Line.* (no date)

——. *Series 7 Diesel-Electric Locomotives.* Erie, Pa., 1980.

——. *Achieving a Leadership Position in Turbocharger Technology.* Erie, Pa., 1982.

——. *A New Generation for Increased Productivity.* Erie, Pa., 1984.

——. *A New Generation for Increased Productivity.* Erie, Pa., 1987.

——. *GE Diesel Engines—Power for Progress.* Erie, Pa., 1988.

——. *GENESIS Series.* 1993.

Periodicals

Baldwin Locomotives. Philadelphia, Pa. (no longer published)

CTC Board. Ferndale, Washington.

Diesel Era. Halifax, Pa.

Diesel Railway Traction, supplement to *Railway Gazette* (UK). (merged into *Railway Gazette*)

Jane's World Railways. London.

Modern Railways. Surrey, U.K.

Official Guide to the Railways. New York.

Pacific RailNews. Waukesha, Wis. (no longer published)

Passenger Train Journal. Waukesha, Wis. (no longer published)

Railroad History, formerly *Railway and Locomotive Historical Society Bulletin.* Boston, Mass.

Railway Age, Chicago and New York.

TRAINS Magazine. Waukesha, Wis.

Vintage Rails. Waukesha, Wis. (no longer published)

INDEX